ADULT
CRIME
and
SOCIAL
POLICY

PRENTICE-HALL SERIES IN SOCIAL POLICY

Howard E. Freeman, Editor

Daniel Glaser

ADULT
CRIME
and
SOCIAL
POLICY

prentice-hall, inc.
englewood cliffs, new jersey

PREFACE

Crime is frequently called America's most important domestic problem. Whether it deserves more attention than poverty, race relations, or other issues could well be questioned. Public opinion polls repeatedly demonstrate, however, that it is a major source of concern.

Most generalizations on crime as a whole are false, simply because the term "crime" denotes too wide a variety of events to be described or explained by a single label. One preoccupation of this book is, therefore, to identify the types and dimensions of crime most relevant to social policy, and to make statements specific to each. Our title and opening chapter refer to age as a crucial dimension partly because societal machinery for coping with crime differs according to whether the offender is juvenile or adult, and partly because the social changes that occur in the transition from childhood to adulthood are causally related to much crime. These and other causal processes which must be considered when attempting to explain and prevent crime are discussed in Chapters 2 and 3.

Police, courts, and corrections are three diverse types of social organization for interrupting criminal careers. In their day-to-day activities, officials in these organizations have the additional concerns of reducing their work, enhancing their status, and making their jobs secure. How these various endeavors interact and what their impact is on efforts to prevent crime and to change offenders are discussed in the last three chapters of this book.

I am indebted to Professors Frank J. Remington and Herman Goldstein of the University of Wisconsin Law School for helpful comments on a first draft for Chapters 4 and 5. A major part of what clarity and stylistic merit this book may possess is due to my wife Pearl's innumerable constructive criticisms and suggestions for rephrasing. Any deficiencies in the book we blame on our scapedog Pixie.

DANIEL GLASER

University of Southern California

CONTENTS

CRIME AND ADULTHOOD, 1   Chapter **1**

   Defining Crime by Status   1
   Defining Crime by Behavior   2
   The Relationship between Crime and Age   4

CAUSAL PROCESSES   **2**
IN ADULT CRIME, 8

   From Adolescence to Adulthood   8
   Problems in Classifying Criminal Careers   12
   Some Guidelines in Differentiating Criminal Careers
   for Social Policy Purposes   14

      A. Offense Descriptive Variables, 15
      B. Career Commitment Variables, 19

TEN POLICY-RELEVANT TYPIFICATIONS   **3**
OF ADULT CRIME CAREERS, 27

   Adolescence Recapitulators   28
   Subcultural Assaulters   32
   Addiction-Supporting Predators   37

Vocational Predators 44
Organized Illegal Sellers 47
Avocational Predators 56
Crisis-Vacillation Predators 58
Quasi-Insane Assaulters 59
Addicted Performers 62
Private Illegal Consumers 64

THE POLICE, 67 **4**

The Atomization of American Police Power 67
The Multiplicity of Police Concerns 69
Police-Public Relationships 75

THE COURTS, 80 **5**

Arrest and the Right to a Hearing 82
Initial Appearance: Right to Counsel 82
Initial Appearance: Confirmation of Arrest 84
Initial or Subsequent Appearances: Bail-Setting 87
Continuances 91
Preliminary Hearing, Grand Jury,
and Indictment or Information 94
The Trial and Trial Jury 95
Conclusion on Courts 98

CORRECTION, 100 **6**

Sentencing Variations 100
Correctional Goals and Procedures 102
Guiding Correctional Policy 109

SELECTED REFERENCES, 112

INDEX, 123

ADULT
CRIME
and
SOCIAL
POLICY

Chapter 1

CRIME AND ADULTHOOD

In the twentieth century, becoming a criminal and becoming an adult are experiences related both by legal definitions and by causal influences. These relationships must be known and understood if one is to guide social policy effectively. This chapter will summarize definitional and statistical aspects of crime and their bearing on age. Later chapters will deal with causal processes in the genesis of crime, and assess efforts to control or prevent crime.

Defining Crime by Status

Crime is defined legally as any behavior for which the state may lawfully punish an individual. It should be noted, however, that whether a governmental agency can officially punish a person for his behavior depends upon the person's status. Formerly, people could not be lawfully punished by the state for some acts if they were of the nobility or clergy, but could be punished if they were commoners. Today, the kind of status that most frequently restricts the state in inflicting punishment is age.

The legal definition of a person whom the state may punish includes the requirement that he be an adult. The ancient legal principle of *nonage* specified a birthday before which a person's behavior was not a lawful basis for punishment by the state. In most British-American legal history, adulthood simply meant being above this age, which used to be seven years but now varies from ten to fourteen depending on the state. Among the Puritans of our seventeenth century Massachusetts Bay Colony, people were sometimes put in the stocks or even hanged when only eleven or twelve years old.

At the beginning of the twentieth century the legal nonage distinction of adult from child became blurred by the concept of *juvenile delinquency*. This was premised on the belief that when someone under a specified age commits a crime it is an indication that he has received improper parental training or supervision. A special "juvenile court" to which such a case is referred can then declare that instead of receiving the penalty prescribed by law for the offense, the youth will be made a ward of the state. The state is supposed to serve as wise parent when real parents fail or are not available. This is the principle of *parens patriae,* or of the state's acting as parent. Under this principle the court can impose any of a large variety of restrictions on the juvenile and on his or her parents according to what the judge deems appropriate to the prevention of further delinquency. (For an intensive history, but perhaps hypercritical evaluation of this development, see Platt, 1969.)

Juvenile delinquency is any behavior committed by a person under a certain age which would be considered crime if he were older, as well as diverse behavior deemed by the court to be conducive to crime, such as unauthorized absence from home or school, impudence towards parents or teachers, or even drinking or smoking. After the upper age limit of delinquent status—which in most states is eighteen, but is sixteen or seventeen in several—one may absent oneself from home or school or be impudent to parents without being liable to court-imposed penalties. Because one's status in terms of age makes such a difference, these types of delinquency have been called *juvenile status offenses* by criminologists Thorsten Sellin and Marvin Wolfgang (1964).

Defining Crime by Behavior

Since crime is any behavior for which a court may lawfully impose punishment, that which is called crime varies somewhat from one state to the next, and from one period of time to another. The acts widely punished as crime today can be classified into five major categories, some of which have long been regarded as criminal almost everywhere, while others have received diverse treatment in different legal jurisdictions and at various times.

Predatory crimes or *predations* are what we most commonly think of as crime. They are acts in which a person deliberately takes or injures someone else's person or property. Their creation of definite and intended victims distinguishes them from the four other major types of lawfully punishable behavior in our classification system. Predation may be divided into two broad sub-categories, crimes against persons and crimes against property.

Crimes against persons and their legal definitions stated briefly are primarily the following:

> *Murder*—deliberate killing.
>
> *Simple Assault*—a physical attack creating no threat of serious injury.
>
> *Aggravated Assault* or *Assault and Battery*—an attack involving attempt to inflict or actual infliction of severe bodily injury, or attempt to kill.
>
> *Kidnapping*—the confining or transporting of a person against his will.
>
> *Rape*—the use of force or threat of force to have sexual intercourse with a woman without her consent.
>
> *Sexual Molestation* or *Indecent Liberties*—unsolicited sexually motivated acts towards another person, not involving intercourse (and usually toward children).

If a woman is below the "age of consent," usually set by law as sixteen, sexual intercourse with her is called "rape" even if she freely cooperated or even seduced the male, but it is generally distinguished as *statutory rape*.

Crimes against property include:

> *Theft* or *Larceny*—taking someone else's property. (*Grand* or *Petty* theft or larceny are distinguished according to whether the value of the property taken is more or less than a specified amount, usually $50).
>
> *Burglary*—breaking into and entering a building in order to commit any crime (but usually done to commit theft).
>
> *Robbery*—taking someone's property by force or threat of force. (In a sense it is a crime against both person and property).
>
> *Fraud*—taking someone's property by deceit.

The most frequently prosecuted of the many varieties of fraud is *forgery,* the preparation or alteration of a document—usually a check—in order to obtain money to which one is not entitled. *Embezzlement* is a violation of trust to defraud someone, for example, a bookkeeper's alteration of accounts in order to appropriate his employer's money for his personal use. *Confidence Games* or *"bunco"* consist of misrepresentation in order to defraud, as when the victim is led to believe that he is paying for some goods or services, but the seller has no intention of conveying them to him.

The major forms of *predation* are punished by the state in all countries of appreciable social and cultural complexity, at least in all which have monetary and banking systems. Unlike predation, however, the other four major types of crime we distinguish here are not universally and consistently defined as crime. *Illegal selling* and *illegal consumption* involve collaboration by the participants, and thus are intentional but victimless in the sense that the persons punished as criminals—whether for selling or for buying, possessing or using—do not consider themselves victims since they willingly seek the illegal transactions. Perhaps the oldest illegal selling

Crime and Adulthood

offense is the most ancient of professions, *prostitution,* or the sale of sexual favors. Sometimes the state has no penalty for the purchaser of these services, and there are countries in which even the seller is not criminal when licensed by the state. Other illegal selling involves commerce in narcotics, gambling service or untaxed alcoholic beverages. Illustrative of variability in the selling called illegal is the Eighteenth Amendment to the U.S. Constitution, which made it a crime to sell alcoholic beverages, and the Twenty-first Amendment fourteen years later, which made it legal again. In most of the United States the sale of gambling services is legal at the race tracks but not elsewhere, although in some states, notably Nevada, it is legal almost everywhere. Because it is difficult to catch a person in selling or consuming narcotics, the law usually makes mere possession of these substances a crime, except where specifically licensed for medical or research purposes.

Still another broad category of crime is *illegal performance.* This is any behavior which the state can lawfully punish only when the behavior offends an audience, even though it may involve no deliberate intent to offend. The most frequent ground for arrest in the United States is *public drunkenness.* One can be intoxicated as much as one desires without thereby committing a crime if one is not in public. *Indecent exposure, vagrancy,* and *disorderly conduct* are other varieties of illegal performance.

A final major category of crime today is *criminal negligence.* These crimes have unintended victims or potential victims. They are most commonly committed in automobiles, as in *reckless driving, speeding,* and *reckless homicide* or *manslaughter by negligence.*[1] The latter may also be committed by careless construction of buildings or bridges or by improper airplane flying. New forms of criminal negligence develop as technology expands. For example, one form of criminal negligence can be the operation of a radio transmitter in a manner which interferes with other radio communication.

The relationships among the five major categories of crime with respect to the defining variables of criminal intent, definite victim, and relevance of an audience is summarized in Table 1.1.

The Relationship Between Crime and Age

During the twentieth century, agencies for dealing with delinquency have steadily grown more distinct from those dealing with adult crime. It is because of this separation of police, court, corrections,

---

[1] *Criminal homicide,* often referred to only as "homicide," is a term encompassing both *murder,* or intentional killing, and *manslaughter,* which is killing that is unintentional but results from a predatory act such as assault, or from negligence. There is also non-criminal homicide, including that which is deemed "justifiable," as in self-defense, and that which is called "accidental," as occurring unintentionally and despite reasonable precautions.

TABLE 1.1

Victims, Intent, and Dependence on an Audience in the Legal Distinctions of the Major Categories of Crime

Defining Features	Is Criminal Regardless of Audience		Is Criminal Only if it Offends an Audience
	Result of Criminal Intent	Not Result of Criminal Intent	
Has Definite Victims	Predation	Criminal Negligence	Illegal Performance
Does Not Have Definite Victims	Illegal Selling and Illegal Consumption	NOT CRIME	

and prevention activities for adult crime from those for juvenile delinquency that a policy discussion on adult crime may properly be somewhat separate from one on juvenile delinquency. In terms of understanding predatory, illegal selling, illegal consuming, or illegal performing behavior, however, whether the person involved is below or above an age specified in the law is not important. To understand most adult crime one must be familiar with the behavior of the criminal when he was of juvenile age. In fact, the age boundary between delinquency and adult crime in most states, the eighteenth birthday, is close to the median age at arrest for the most frequent predatory offenses. Over half the arrests for burglary and theft are of persons under eighteen.

The age distribution of crime differs considerably for different offenses. Table 1.2 reveals that most crimes against property are predominantly a teenage enterprise, while crimes against persons are more often committed by men in their twenties. However, those who commit fraud are usually somewhat older. Illegal sales and consumption offenses are most frequently committed by still older persons, with the exception of prostitution, where youth enhances sales appeal. Illegal performance offenses, especially drunkenness and disorderly conduct, are primarily the acts of much older persons, with the median age of arrest over forty years.

It should be noted that the official crime data summarized in Table 1.2 is far from a complete and precise tabulation of the legally punishable acts in the United States. Interviews with representative samples of the U.S. population—to ascertain if anyone in their households had been the victim of a predatory offense in the preceding year, and if so, whether it was reported to the police—revealed that about half the seven major predatory

TABLE 1.2

Age of Arrest for Various Offenses in the United States, 1969

Crimes	Number of Offenses Known to Police, in Thousands	Number of Arrests, in Thousands	Median Age of Arrestees	Under 18	Percentage by Age Group			50 and Over
					18–24	25–29	30–49	
Against Persons								
Murder	14.6	11.5	27.4	9	33	16	32	9
Forcible rape	36.5	14.4	22.3	20	45	15	18	2
Aggravated assault	306.4	113.7	26.0	16	31	15	31	7
Other assault	n.a.*	259.8	26.2	18	29	15	32	6
Against Property								
Auto theft	871.9	125.7	17.3	58	30	6	6	1
Other theft								
(over $50)	1512.9	510.7	17.6	53	25	6	12	4
Burglary	1949.8	255.9	17.6	54	30	7	8	1
Robbery	297.6	76.5	19.0	33	43	11	11	1
Forgery and								
counterfeit	n.a.*	36.7	23.5	11	41	18	27	3
Embezzlement	n.a.*	6.3	29.1	4	31	18	40	7
Other fraud	n.a.*	63.4	28.9	5	29	20	40	6
Illegal sales								
Prostitution**	n.a.*	46.4	22.9	2	56	20	18	3
Gambling**	n.a.*	78.0	39.7	2	13	12	47	26
Narcotics**	n.a.*	232.7	19.4	25	53	11	11	1
Illegal Performance								
Drunkenness	n.a.*	1420.2	41.7	3	14	8	47	28
Disorderly conduct	n.a.*	573.5	23.2	20	32	11	28	9
Vagrancy	n.a.*	106.3	27.9	10	33	11	30	16
Negligence								
Manslaughter								
by negligence	n.a.*	3.2	27.6	8	37	15	28	12

(Source: Federal Bureau of Investigation, *Crime in the U.S.: Uniform Crime Reports,* 1969, Washington, D.C.: U.S. Government Printing Office, August, 1970).
        *Not available. Offenses known to police are only compiled by the F.B.I. for its seven "Index Crimes," all predations with relatively high probabilities of victims reporting the offenses to the police, although there may still be a majority not reported in all but murder and auto theft.
        **Includes some arrests for illegal consumption.

crimes which the Federal Bureau of Investigation calls "Index Offenses" (those for which figures are available in the first column of Table 1.2) are never reported to the police (President's Commission, 1967, pp. 20–22). In addition, police recording and tabulation of crimes reported to them has never been complete.

   The only crimes for which statistics are fairly complete are homicide, auto theft, and bank robbery. Much robbery, burglary, and theft are not reported to the police by the victims because they do not believe the police can solve the crimes, because they do not want to be involved in testifying in court, because they know the offender as a relative or neighbor, or for other reasons. Only a small fraction of assaults and rapes are reported to the police because it is often very humiliating to talk of these experiences, and because the criminals usually are not strangers to the victims. It is probable that a major part of the alleged increase in crime rates in recent years can be attributed to a larger percentage being reported to the police, and to the police keeping more complete records than heretofore. (For a fuller discussion of crime measurement problems and their solution see Glaser, 1967.)

Identifying and measuring crime are but the first steps to its understanding and control. The next step is to trace its genesis in order to infer its causes.

Chapter 2

CAUSAL PROCESSES IN ADULT CRIME

To explain adult crime we must relate it to its antecedents. This requires that we describe the emergence of criminal activity and identify criminogenic conditions in the life histories of individuals from early childhood on. Explanation also requires that we distinguish between types of criminal activity which result from different causal processes.

From Adolescence to Adulthood

Adolescence is the period of life which begins with puberty and ends when the social roles of adulthood are acquired—the period between childhood and adulthood. The rate of crime has always been high in this transition period. In today's society it may well be higher than ever, because the duration of adolescence grows increasingly longer as the age for beginning adult roles becomes greater and the average age of physical maturity has slightly declined. Indeed, a more prolonged and socially separated adolescence may be the major cause of high crime rates in the United States.

At one time, most youths took full-time jobs shortly after reaching physical maturity at which time they began employment at unskilled work in which their earnings might equal or exceed those of older men in the same line of work. For others the transition to adult roles was more gradual, as when they became apprentices to skilled tradesmen and were only later given full adult responsibilities. In either case, their roles were closely integrated with those of adults. But this continuity between the activities of youth and older people dwindled as society increasingly required a longer span of education prior to adult employment, and as conditions of life made adolescent and adult social circles more separate.

Adolescents today are more removed from adults—physically and socially—than they were in previous eras. More of them than ever before complete junior and senior high school, and attend college. In these years they are largely segregated from adults—as well as from young children— except for maintaining what is usually a rather impersonal relationship to teachers. Indeed, student life at these school levels separates age groups more today than formerly because the schools are larger and more specialized, and because their curricular and extra-curricular activities absorb a larger fraction of the student's day. Even during many of the hours when not at school, however, adolescents are separated from adults more than when in school, and more than formerly was customary, because more mothers of adolescents now work away from home. The return of mothers to the labor market when their children reach adolescence is facilitated by modern household appliances, as well as by easily cared-for clothing and pre- processed foods which reduce the toil in "keeping house." Also, there are now fewer chores for all age levels in the family to perform together because there are fewer family businesses such as farms or small shops in which all ages once worked as a group.

A basic law of sociology and anthropology is that social separation results in cultural differentiation. As adolescents live apart from other age groups, their norms of speech, dress, musical taste, and morality become different from those of adults. Because the borderlines of adolescence are not clearly defined, there is much conflict between them and adults as to which norms are proper. In this conflict of generations, the adolescent seeks the independence in determing his own behavior which characterizes adult status, but he is not given such autonomy as long as he is deemed not ready for economic independence. Youths are usually not economically self-supporting as early as they once were, but they are socially on their own to a greater extent than ever.

In the separate adolescent world striving for acceptance or even respect and leadership makes somewhat different demands than are required for success in school or in social interaction with adults. The youth who is unsuccessful in meeting the performance standards of his school may often compensate by achieving prestige among his peers. (This is well demon- strated in Coleman, 1961.)

When adolescents engage in behavior that is deviant by adult standards they must be especially secretive, and this lack of communication makes their cultural norms differ even more from those of adults. One indicator of this divergence is the contrasting experience of age groups with respect to drugs. A survey of the New York state population in 1968 indicated that 58 percent of males aged seventeen through nineteen personally knew someone who had used marijuana in the preceding year, whereas only 8 percent of those over forty years old had such knowledge (Glaser and Snow, 1969). No other variable investigated—including neighborhood, race, sex, income, education, or religion—differentiated the population in familiarity with drug use nearly as much as age did.

For the adolescent in conflict with adults because they regard his behavior as unsatisfactory, achievement in the adolescent world is especially appealing. Much truancy from school, vandalism, auto theft for joyriding, and other delinquency expresses a flaunting of independence from adult control. Theft of desired things, or of money to purchase them, further decreases dependence on adults. Adolescent drinking, drug use and sexual activity give boys a sense of manhood and girls that accompany them a sense of independence and sophistication in attracting and pleasing men.

While most juvenile delinquency is outgrown with no great jeopardy to normative conformity in adult life, sometimes it is highly conducive to future criminal behavior. This depends on how a youth's delinquency affects his seeking and obtaining satisfying and legitimate employment when he becomes an adult. Juvenile delinquency's influence on adult careers has two mechanisms. The juvenile who finds immediate rewards in predatory crime or illegal selling prefers it to studies or to legitimate employment. Thus he becomes progressively more skilled and socially involved in unlawful occupations and less qualified or interested in "respectable" jobs. Conversely, if he is unsuccessful at his illegitimate activities and is caught, the punishment and stigma that result may severely impede his being accepted in legitimate roles. Being labelled criminal as a youth may mean rejection from school and from law-abiding associates or potential employers, thereby increasing the relative attractiveness of criminal over legitimate pursuits.

It should be noted that the low median age of arrests for predation, and the fact that most adults admit having committed crimes when younger, mean that only a minority of the persons who commit predations as adolescents will develop predatory careers as adults. Most people, youths and adults alike, try to hide their deviant activity from persons who regard them as conforming to prevailing norms. A youth's ties with family, teachers, employers, and others are usually sufficient for him to attempt to preserve a "good reputation." Therefore, most youths cease deviant activity when it might jeopardize their reputations. Their most common reaction to being labelled criminal is not to risk further criminality (Briar and Piliavin, 1965). It is when social rewards for being a conforming person cannot compete successfully with the gratifications of crime that the latter are avidly pursued.

A person's anticipation of success in either deviant or conforming activities is, in large part, a function of the relative degree of prior success he has had in each. The earlier he is successful in delinquent activities, the more likely he is to become preoccupied with such pursuits. As a result, his experience of success in legitimate endeavors will decrease. That is why truancy from school is one of the best statistical predictors of later delinquency (Glaser, 1962), and why recidivism of criminals at any age varies inversely with their age at their first arrest (Glaser and O'Leary, 1966). In crime as in other behavior, learning is a function of the reinforcements experienced.

Anticipation of the consequences of his behavior varies, for a reflective man, not only with his past reinforcements, but also, according to his perception of future contingencies. These perceptions fluctuate in both criminal and non-criminal careers because they are affected by past commitments. As Becker (1960) points out, commitments are a matter of prior assertions and social involvements. If a person has "put up a front" and gained a "rep" as a "tough," a clever thief, or a sophisticated drug user, he may worry about losing "face" and friends should he abandon toughness, theft, or drug use. If, however, he has a reputation and a satisfying self-conception as a "decent and respectable citizen" or a "dependable employee," he knows that he places these in jeopardy should he engage in crime.

Both a criminal and a conforming life generate anxiety. A person may risk arrest, long confinement, sickness from drug use, or injury from gunshot when he ventures into crime. If he suffers any of these—or is frightened by a "close call" with them—he is likely to contemplate "going straight." A non-criminal life usually is disturbed less dramatically than that of a criminal, but it may be upset by such developments as failure at a job, poor budgetting, bad luck, marital strife, or personality afflictions such as alcoholism.

Crime is often perceived by previously noncriminal persons as a short-cut to the resolution of their tensions, just as it is perceived by adolescents as a short-cut to the independence of adulthood. That is why diverse ages and prior life styles are at times associated with the initiation of criminal careers, even though so many begin with adolescent delinquency. As a rule, commitment increases with duration of criminal or noncriminal pursuits, but tensions are always possible which may suffice to destroy all accumulated commitments.

What has been implied thus far is that an understanding of the causal processes in adult crime often requires a tracing of the life histories of individual criminals from early youth to reveal the turning points in their careers and to relate these to antecedent and concurrent events. It has also been implied that the patterns of criminal careers are extremely diverse. A first step in furthering understanding is the classification of these patterns into major types. That is the concern of the rest of this chapter and of Chapter 3. A further step is to relate these types to social policies, especially those of agencies for dealing with crime—that will be the concern of the remainder of this book.

Problems in Classifying Criminal Careers

Though the variety of behavior that may be called crime is immense, it was possible in Chapter 1 to reduce it to five broad categories. Within each category, however, several separate types were indicated, and those mentioned were far from an exhaustive list. To differentiate criminal careers one might try to take into account not only all possible combinations of types of crime committed in the course of each career, but also the sequence in which they were committed, the age of the offender when committing them, whether he engaged in them alone or with others, his personality or motives, his family, class or ethnic background, his area of residence, his skill or style at crime, and innumerable other variables. Obviously, every separate career will be seen as unique if classified by enough categories, and the number of logical ways of grouping the careers of separate individuals into a limited set of types is probably infinite. For this reason, a large variety of criminal typologies are found in the literature (many are described in Clinard and Quinney, 1967, Chapter One, and in Driver, 1968).

Typification is the first step in the interpretation of experience. Psychologically, it is what differentiates perception from sensation. To ascribe meaning to experience we must perceive it as having separate components, then classify these components to indicate a relationship among them. Our classifications are based on what we have learned previously, and on our purpose. Thus a man who has not learned the botanist's taxonomies cannot classify a mushroom by its technical name, but even if he could, he might only wish to know if it were edible or poisonous. Prevailing criminal typologies vary according to the purposes of the classifiers, for example, whether they wish to formulate a theory to explain crime, to prescribe policy for dealing with offenders, or to distinguish among criminal self-conceptions. Some typologies reflect multiple purposes.

Another aspect of classifying is perception of differences as discrete or continuous. Thus, people are usually discretely categorized as male or female, and if they are examined closely enough, there is no disagreement as to their sex. On the other hand, height is a continuous variable. If asked to designate males as either tall or short, classifiers can agree on individuals who illustrate each of these terms, but they will disagree on how to classify the many people intermediate between the extremes. This will be resolved only if they are instructed to apply some arbitrary rule, such as that everyone five feet nine inches tall or over shall be called "tall" and all others "short."

This example of height illustrates what occurs in many typologies of criminal careers that appear in the literature. These employ continuous dimensions but present them as discrete dichotomies, such as "occasional" or "habitual," "naïve" or "professional," and "specialized" or "non-specialized." Readers will accept selected cases as illustrative of each side of these dichotomies, but finding an illustrative case, no matter how rare, is as far as many writers go in checking their typologies empirically. If they applied them to a cross-section of a prison or other large criminal population, they would find most cases intermediate between the illustrated extremes of such dichotomous types. Therefore, arbitrary rules must be created to apply these typological variables. The variables are most valid if divided into several ranges—such as "high," "medium" and "low"—but if they cannot be measured precisely, each new cutting point to distinguish a separate range creates a new set of borderline cases that will not be classified consistently.

The cause of such problems in typification has long been familiar in philosophy; in explaining things we begin by idealizing them, that is, we conceive of them as less complex and variegated than they are in fact (Lopreato and Alston, 1970). By focusing on extreme cases we can often make more plausible explanations for a phenomenon, but if these types are the extremes of a continuous dimension with most cases in the real world intermediate between them, the typology may be of very limited practical utility. Conceiving of contrasting types, however, even if unrealistic, may be the first step towards identifying and measuring new and salient dimensions along which all cases can be continuously differentiated.

A further difficulty with many typologies is that each conceived type represents a unique combination of several variables, but in a cross-section of cases these combinations may be rare. As Winch (1947) has pointed out, there are essentially two approaches to distinguishing multivariate types. The *heuristic* is by the idealization process, and is derived from some kind of theory. It consists of not paying attention to all variability in individuals, but focusing on those attributes that several seem to share, and for which the classifier has an explanation. The other method is *empirical*: one measures all cases by certain variables and makes statistical tabulations and calculations to determine which traits cluster together. As Winch observed:

> Empirical typologies can correct errors in heuristic typologies, can reveal types where none has been posited or suspected, and can provide a basis for 'integrating' various disciplines. Empirical typologies are especially useful where the problem area is new, where the extant theory seems inadequate, and where it seems desirable to attempt a transdisciplinary approach. [1947]

Social types are idealizations that have become part of a culture or subculture. The term *stereotyping* refers, essentially, to the tendency towards idealization in the way people think about others. Social types, to classify people according to their key differences, develop from observations that are idealized through myths or through stereotyping to generalize about many people as though they were all alike. The "cowboy," the "pirate," the "gladhander," the "corrupt politician," the "social climber" and the various ethnic labels expressing prejudice each connotes to those who use them a fairly specific set of personality attributes. Users of these terms share similar images of the personalities so labelled, although their images are often erroneous.

Many typologies by criminologists have tried to capture the social typification in the speech of criminals. Irwin (1970), for example, mixed examples of inmate speech with his own descriptions, when he classified the careers of 116 California prison releasees as "Thief," "Hustler," "Dope Fiend," "Head," "Disorganized Criminal," "State-raised Youth," "Lower Class 'Man'" and "Square John." In describing roles of prison inmates (which may not necessarily correspond to total career patterns), Sykes (1958) explicitly described the types as *argot roles*, suggesting that the function of these labels is to call attention to aspects of the behavior of other prisoners which are important for the distinctions inmates must make in dealing with them. Sykes found that prisoners classified each other with regard to homosexuality as "wolves," "fags," or "punks," and in terms of nonsexual aggressive tendencies as "ball-busters," "hipsters," "toughs" and "gorillas." That these are idealizations of continuous and mixed dimensions is evident when one asks inmates to apply these terms to specific persons. They will agree on specific illustrations, but will disagree or use qualifying terms to denote relativity if asked to classify everyone in a particular prison unit. They will say: "He's a bit of a 'wolf,' but not as much as Bill is," or "He's sometimes a 'gorilla' and sometimes a 'right guy'" (see Glaser and Stratton, 1961, at 383–386).

In the real world, the gradations and mixtures of characteristics in people are so extensive that most of our categories must be given very arbitrary boundaries if everyone in a cross-section of the population is to be placed in one empirical type or another. Most real people just do not fall neatly into uniform patterns. Therefore, we formulate explanations in terms of idealizations, we revise them on the basis of research on empirical types, and in the practical world we qualify most explanations for separate cases to meet the variations we encounter beyond what any set of type labels denote.

Some Guidelines in Differentiating Criminal Careers for Social Policy Purposes

The preceding discussion of problems in typification highlights the limitations in all typologies current in criminological literature, as well as the typology presented in the next chapter of this book. One must deal with the diversity of the criminal world, nevertheless, by sorting it on whatever variables seem to improve the fit of our causal generalizations to reality, even though a perfect fit is impossible.

For policy guidance purposes it is important to describe criminal careers both by *offense descriptive* variables—which identify the problem a career creates for society—and by *career commitment* variables—which suggest the strategies needed to prevent criminal careers from developing, or to alter them once they have begun. The following are brief descriptions of some variables of both types most relevant to social policy, together with an indication of the reasons for their relevance, and of problems in applying them to make empirical distinctions.

A. OFFENSE DESCRIPTIVE VARIABLES

Some of these were already used in classifying types of crime for Chapter 1. They are supplemented here both by additional distinctions of style of crime performance, and by some discussion of the problem of classifying the combinations of separate crimes that an individual engages in during the course of his career.

1. Predatory or Non-Predatory. This initial dichotomy separates crimes according to whether they have a definite and intended victim or not. It is discrete and usually—but not always—unambiguous. It is important for social policy purposes, because a victim (or his friend or relative) has an interest in reporting a crime to the police, and this facilitates its being known and acted upon by government agencies. With non-predatory crimes, enforcement and even assessment of the problem is greatly impaired by the fact that few persons observing or affected by the offenses have a strong motivation to report them. In practice, however, as was indicated in Chapter 1, even predatory crimes are not always reported, particularly those other than murder, auto theft or bank robbery.

2. Person or Property Predations. This is the same distinction made in Chapter 1—between predators who attack the persons of their victims and those who take their property by stealth or deceit. The values of our society make a person-property distinction important for social policy purposes, since crimes against persons are usually considered much more serious public concerns than crimes against property. This dichotomy becomes important also because of its relationship to commitment variables; money (or property in lieu of money) is a general reinforcer for behavior, and crimes against property are alternatives to all conventional economic pursuits, but crimes against persons have diverse behavior reinforcement functions, many quite difficult to comprehend.

Person or property is a discrete variable, but has some ambiguities. For example, most robbery seems to be primarily a crime against property, for financial gain seems to be the sole motive. This is clear in many holdups in which the gun is not loaded, or is even a toy gun or any object in the pocket which looks like a gun. When force has priority, however, as in the behavior of some muggers who attack first and continue even when their victim is not resisting or is unconscious, the offense could more properly be called a crime against the person even though property is taken. Arson, a less frequent crime, is also sometimes ambiguous. It is often an offense against property, as when it is committed to defraud an insurance company; occasionally it is an expression of hostility against an agency or person; sometimes it is done without intent to injure or gain so much as to obtain some peculiar psychological satisfaction from watching a fire. Recently, some arson, bombing, and assault has been directed against presumed symbols of political or economic policy, as a political protest.

3. Selling, Consuming, Performing, or Negligent Offenses. This four-fold classification, applied only to non-predatory offenses, is nearly exhaustive, and is fairly unambiguous. These four divisions are important for social policy because they involve different role relationships, and therefore, control of each has requirements and consequences different from those for control of the others.

Someone engaged in illegal selling of a commodity must develop relationships with both suppliers and buyers (but with only the latter if selling a personal service, as the prostitute, not employed by a panderer or a brothel). A seller's volume of trade depends upon his being known to potential buyers; he is handicapped if he must operate secretly. When dealing in commodities, or in a large gambling operation, his investment losses may be great if his operations are stopped. Therefore, it is profitable for sellers to invest large sums in corrupting the police and perhaps other government officials if this permits them to operate more openly. Corrupt police and other officials thus have a licensing and insurance function for organized crime (see Gardner and Olson, 1967). Illegal selling is often run by an extensive organization rather than by an individual acting alone; the business is most efficient and secure if it has much capital and many specialists in buying, selling, corrupting, and other required activities, all closely coordinated. Because these are illegal business organizations, they have their own rule-enforcement staff, who may assault, rob, kidnap, or murder not only competitors, but also some members of their own organization, or potential witnesses in legal efforts to convict them. These features, plus the fact that they may accumulate immense wealth and develop vast powers to corrupt legitimate business as well as government, cause them to pose distinctive social policy problems (Cressey, 1969).

Consuming offenses usually require some relationships with a few members of a trafficking organization, but not with all of its specialists. Usually the users of an illegal service or commodity operate alone or in small and informal cliques rather than in large organizations. From a policy standpoint, illegal consumption crimes highlight the difficulties of law enforcement against private activities. There is a danger that these difficulties may lead to a breakdown of due process norms in law enforcement through use of informers, entrapment, unwarranted searches, and "no-knock" entries. They also reflect cultural cleavage within society as noted in the discussion of adolescent-adult differences, and the prospect of a weakening of many types of norms due to the self-segregation of generations which this cleavage promotes.

Performing, selling, and consuming offenses pose policy questions because of variability in their public definition both as deviance and as crime. For example, the styles of public dress which resulted in prosecution for indecent exposure several decades ago included the male's being barechested and the female's exposing the upper thigh, but such exposure is now increasingly customary in many public situations. (It was never illegal in private circumstances.)

Criminal negligence is a social policy problem quite different from any of the other types of crime distinguished here. High correlation of negligent driving with other types of criminality, however, has been demonstrated (Eysenck, 1964, 19–21; Babst, *et al,* 1969). This suggests that traditional emphasis on psychological causes of negligence should be supplemented by investigations of subcultural values. Regardless, safety engineering, patrolling, inspecting, and educating seem to be the public policy measures most closely related to the reduction of negligence rates.

4. Residual Crime Descriptions. While crime was dichotomized as predatory or non-predatory in our first variable, and additional divisions were made thereafter, it should be stressed that many further typifications of crime are relevant to both causal analysis and social policy.

Predations against persons may be differentiated as hostile, sexual, or financial in motivation, and sometimes as combinations of these. Sexual predations may be differentiated as directed towards children or adults, or as heterosexual or homosexual. They may also be differentiated as passive or aggressive—the most passive being voyeurism or peeping, from which the suffering of the alleged victim may be so negligible that the act might well be called an illegal consumption rather than a predation. This is of social policy interest because, contrary to widespread fears, peepers practically never shift to aggressive sexual predation. Still further distinctions among both predatory and non-predatory sex offenders were usefully made in the exhaustive studies of the Institute for Sex Research of Indiana University founded by the scientific pioneer of this field, the late Alfred C. Kinsey (Gebhard, *et al,* 1965).

Predations against property were classified in Chapter 1 by major legal categories of theft, burglary, robbery, forgery, embezzlement, and the confidence game. Theft is legally differentiated as petty or grand, with most criminal codes making auto theft a separate category. Other useful distinctions not always made in the law include shoplifting, pocket picking, and "car clouting" (theft from autos), each of which is often a career specialty for appreciable durations of life span.

Criminalists, the scientific crime detectors, classify all predators by their *modus operandi*. Many of the major differences noted for detection purposes are relevant to causal and policy considerations. Predators can be distinguished as lone or group offenders, and groups can be differentiated by the extent of their division into specified roles, such as "joint-caser" or "finger man," "lookout," "driver," "inside man," and "gun." Forgers, who are usually lone offenders, have been distinguished by Lemert as "naive" or "systematic" (1967, Chapters 7, 8 and 9); the latter are highly professional and mobile deceivers, while the former cash petty checks, usually just enough to maintain drinking escapades interrupted by lack of funds. Similarly, Cameron (1964) has differentiated the professional shoplifter ("booster") from the avocational "snitch." Maurer has itemized a diversity of roles and career patterns in picking pockets (1964) and in confidence games (1940).

Non-predatory crime was divided into selling, consuming, performing, or negligence offenses by the third set of distinctions introduced. Some of the major specialties within each were indicated. All of them can be further differentiated in a manner useful for theory and for practical policy. Prostitutes are commonly divided into "call girls," "street walkers," and "house broads" (Bryan, 1965). Sutter (1969) classified San Francisco users and sellers of illegal drugs as "potheads," "players," "hustlers," and "dope fiends"—and other distinctions have been made elsewhere reflecting drugs used, means of support, and culturally rooted self-conceptions.

5. *Specialization*. This variable distinguishes criminal careers according to whether they consistently involve the same type of crime or diverse types. It is clearly the most difficult descriptive variable to apply. Of course, one has no problem with those who commit only one type of crime, whether it is a broad or a narrow type. According to their specialty we can call them predators, assaulters, thieves, forgers, drug addicts, exhibitionists, or reckless drivers, for example. The difficulty arises from the fact that a large variety of offenses are found in most separate criminal careers, and the combinations occur in all possible proportions. It might seem to be a simple solution to refer to a profile of the proportions of crimes that are of each particular type. In doing this, however, there are problems in determining what is a unit of such crimes as illegal consumption. More important, does one give equal weight to all crimes in the career? Surely it would be ridiculous to describe a career of one hundred offenses as 5 percent murder, 25 percent shoplifting, and 70 percent reckless driving.

Despite such difficulties, it is possible to formulate useful rules for rough classifications of offender careers in terms of the type and degree of offense specialization they demonstrate. Usually the degree of specialization increases with the duration of a career, so a classifier's attention will be focused primarily on later years in the career. Also, it is appropriate for public policy concerns to give greatest weight to those offenses that are generally regarded as most serious; in terms of social concern, murder describes the criminal career in the example above rather than the more frequent reckless driving or shoplifting crimes.

B. CAREER COMMITMENT VARIABLES

To assess the prospects of altering a criminal career one must appraise both an offender's commitment to crime and his commitment to a non-criminal style of life. As indicated earlier, these reflect the reinforcements he has received in each, the tensions he may experience in each, the self-conceptions he values, his sense of obligations to others, and the personality conditions (such as paranoia or addiction) which crime may support.

The measurement of commitment is never a matter of precision. It may be inferred from resistance to efforts to change behavior, from verbal responses to standard questions, or more reliably and validly, from known correlations of persistence in crime with record of past behavior or experience. The following are a few variables demonstrated by research to be statistical indicators of commitment.

1. Prior Criminality. Just as the best predictor of next year's weather in a particular area is the weather of that area in previous years, the best predictor of a person's crime in future years is his crime in past years. With crime as with the weather, such predictions are far from perfect, but rates of persistence in crime are statistically related to the number of previous arrests or convictions, the total span of criminal record, and the total time confined (Glaser and O'Leary, 1966). Presumably these relationships reflect both the fact that arrest and incarceration are correlated with prior criminality, and the possibility that these involvements of offenders with the law were more crime-promoting than rehabilitative experiences. As indicated earlier, rates of persistence in crime are inversely related to age at first arrest—presumably because, for offenders at any specific current age, the earlier their first arrest occurred, the longer was the span of time in which they pursued crime.

It should be noted, however, that careers in crime are frequently interrupted by conventional careers. Unpublished statistical tabulations by Gottfredson and Glaser (in the California and Federal correction systems, respectively) indicate that a prisoner who had five or more years of non-criminal career in the free community before the crime which sent him to prison, but had a criminal record before that, had nearly the same high probability of success on parole as a first offender. Unfortunately, the tabulations did not control for age, and those with an interrupted criminal career were probably older, on the average, than first offenders. This is relevant because rates of persistence in crime diminish with age. Indeed, the increase in rates of parole violation diminishes with the number of prior arrests or convictions—and in some samples even stops at a certain level—thus, those with more than three or four prior felony convictions have about the same parole violation or recidivism rate as those with three or four. Perhaps the ability and willingness to cope with the tensions of a criminal career diminish with age, and possibly the offender's satisfaction in a noncriminal life also increases with age (Glaser and O'Leary, 1966, plus unpublished tabulations).

2. *Prior Source of Income.* The best way to guess how much more income a man has than he indicates on his income tax report is often to compare his reported income with his standard of living and his net worth. Similarly, one of the best ways to assess a man's commitment to crime is to try to infer what his sources of income have been in the past. Proven statistical indices of noncriminality include the duration of the longest period of employment in a particular job held by a person, his total legitimate earnings per year, the percentage of his time in the civilian community during which he was employed when not in school, and the status of the jobs he has had as measured on any reasonable scale (e.g., unskilled, skilled, white collar, professional). The higher on the scale all of these items are, the lower is the percentage of failure on parole (Glaser and O'Leary, 1966). They are indices of prior success at noncriminal alternatives to property predation, and of behavior that usually—though not always—is incompatible with much involvement in crime of any sort. Conversely, the longer the period that an individual had no legitimate source of income, the greater is the probability that he supported himself by crime in that period, regardless of whether or not he was arrested. His rent, recreation, and auto in this period are indices of his total income. An estimate of the probable monetary reinforcement he was obtaining from crime may be inferred by comparing estimates of income from these clues with available evidence on his past earnings from legal sources.

3. *Social Relationships.* The primary sources of a person's pro-criminal or anticriminal commitments, in most cases, are his social relationships. Commitment, as Becker (1960) suggested, is mainly a matter of how one has presented oneself to others, and how one values the impression one makes on them. Intricately involved in this, or identical with it, is the conception one has of oneself.

A first step in using social relationships as an index of commitment to crime is to explore the extent to which others are involved in a person's crime, either as partners or as supporters. Much crime is conducted alone

and secretly. Most systematic forgery and some naïve forgery, most shoplifting by housewives, most embezzlement, most male sexual aggression
against females, and much use of narcotics by physicians, nurses, or pharmacists appear to be done altogether furtively, unknown even to their closest
friends or relatives (Lemert, 1967, Chapters 7, 8 and 9; Cameron, 1964;
Cressey, 1953; Gebhardt, *et al,* 1965, Chapter 9; Winick, 1961). If social
relationships are involved in these crimes it is very indirectly—long before
the crimes occur—through their influence on personality, which in turn
may determine the reinforcement potential of these offenses for the individuals who commit them. Because these offenders do not usually think
of themselves as criminal, all except the forgers have a high probability of
ceasing crime if labelled as criminal and punished or counseled appropriately.
The high rate of persistence in forgery reflects the high rate of immediate
monetary reinforcement it provides, in addition to its frequently being
pursued to support alcoholism.

Social relationships are directly involved in commitment to most other
types of criminal career in one of three different ways. The most familiar,
of course, is a shared socialization in criminal values or even partnership
in crime. This is evident in juvenile gangs and in organizations of adults
for illegal selling. In most property predation there are only a few partners,
such as a two- or three-man holdup or confidence game team. The criminals
may work alone as thieves or burglars, but they know many others in the
same criminal occupation. They develop a few close ties and many acquaintances in correctional institutions, and they have various "hangouts" in
taverns or other places in the outside community. When they meet they
share news of common acquaintances among criminals, exchange advice,
and support each other in rationalizations for crime. In such relationships,
offenders provide each other with encouragement and friendship, and with
pride in their criminal skills, loyalties and reputation which they would be
abandoning should they cease crime.

A second type of social relationship promoting commitment in some
criminal careers is one of conflict. Many adolescent criminals express a
rebelliousness towards parents or other authority figures, and some retain
these emotions in their adult years. Some crimes are committed to spite,
embarrass, injure, or simply to achieve independence from a person against
whom hate, jealousy, or resentment of domination is felt. Such conflict is
not clearly evident in most adult criminal conduct, but it is suggested
dramatically in a few of the more vivid assaultive or destructive offenses.
Indeed, most assaults and even most murders involve two persons who
are friends or relatives—this closeness accounts for the intensity of their
feelings when in conflict.

The third type of social relationship supporting commitment to crime
is symbiotic, such as that between an illegal seller and his customers, or an
illegal consumer and his source of supply. Also symbiotic are the relation-

ships of professional criminals with criminal lawyers, bondsmen, and dealers in stolen goods—"fences." (The latter are also criminal, of course, being a variety of illegal seller.) Each of these aids the other by his transactions, and occasionally acquires some sense of friendship and obligation to the other. Offenders have a higher commitment to crime by virtue of any rewarding relationships they develop in pursuing it.

Affection and obligation towards anticriminal persons, or simply valuing one's reputation among them because one gains material benefits or security from such a reputation, increase commitment to avoiding crime. Married men have lower crime rates than single ones, and married men with children have still lower rates, presumably because of the commitment to conformity that these relationships bring. The criminality of the persons with whom an individual spends his free time, and whom he regards as his friends probably indicates that individual's commitment to crime or to avoiding crime more accurately than anything else, but there are exceptions. Secret crime "to keep up a front" of affluence and generosity with noncriminal friends characterizes many of the lone offenders described at the beginning of this section.

4. Cultural Values. Man's deliberate conduct is always guided by his ideas of what is desirable. We call these ideas his *values.* Everyone is taught values from earliest childhood. Values of honesty, industry, kindliness, and patriotism are emphasized in our social experience as soon as we seem capable of even crudely comprehending them and are repeatedly communicated to us as we grow up.

The values transmitted in a society are as much a part of its culture as its language. Variations in the values emphasized, and sometimes even entirely different values, characterize different subgroups within a society. As already indicated, any group that becomes partially isolated from the rest of society tends to develop a somewhat distinct culture. Variations of the predominant culture are usually called "subcultures," like the adolescent subculture to which earlier discussion alluded.

Subcultural values are sometimes specifically those which are regarded as criminal by the state. For example, during Prohibition the manufacture and sale of whiskey was regarded as legitimate in the regional subculture of the Appalachian hinterlands, and the preparation of homemade wines was approved in the ethnic subcultures of Greek and Italian Americans. Today, the use of psychedelic drugs is highly valued among those who share the "hippie" subculture, while vandalism against schools and, in some circumstances, assault and robbery, are endorsed in delinquent gang subcultures.

It is clear that the intensity of a person's commitment to criminality reflects the extent to which he has been part of a group that had a subculture with values supporting law violation. Conversely, his commitment to noncriminality reflects the extent to which he has been inculcated with values opposing law violation.

5. Personality Traits. The most adequate definition of personality we have been able to devise, to cover all of this term's usage, is: Personality is a description of the regularities in an individual's behavior. Since the future is predicted from the past, description of someone's past behavior as his personality implies a prediction of how that person will behave in the future.

There are so many aspects of behavior one can distinguish that ways of describing personality are infinite. Persistent criminal behavior itself can be the basis for describing someone simply as having a "criminal personality." Psychologists have typed personality by the two methods we have cited from Winch (1947). One is to abstract from behavior those attributes which appear to distinguish individuals, and to coin labels for these such as "extroversion," "introversion," "impulsiveness," and "aggressiveness." This is heuristic typing, in which the attributes are idealized so that behavior is conceived as highly consistent and unambiguous with respect to them. Questions are then devised, or rating sheets for describing another person's behavior are developed, with items which seem to indicate these idealized traits. A person's score on such a collection of items for a given personality trait is then accepted as an index of the extent to which his personality is characterized by that trait.

The second method is empirical typing. One obtains the responses to numerous test items from many individuals and statistically analyzes them to identify the clusters of items that yield the most correlated responses. These correlated items are then presumed to measure a single trait, and a name is given that trait which is taken either from the name of a previous heuristic type which the items seem to describe or newly coined to identify a not previously conceived clustering that the statistical analysis has revealed. An example of the latter is Cattell's "surgency" *vs.* "desurgency" (1965) to designate collectively the correlated items describing people as cheerful or depressed, sociable or seclusive, energetic or languid, witty or dull, talkative or taciturn, and placid or restless.

There is considerable disagreement as to how useful personality measurement can be for assessing commitment to crime. Comparisons of personality test scores of criminals and noncriminals have shown fairly marked and consistent differences only on scales that essentially ask questions about criminal values, for example, the Psychopathic Deviate scale of the Minnesota Multiphasic Personality Inventory and the Socialization scale of Gough's California Personality Inventory (Waldo and Dinitz, 1967). On other aspects of personality measured by verbal or projective tests, criminals are about as diverse as noncriminals, and for most purposes differentiating them by their known criminal or noncriminal behavior appears to be more useful than assessing them on the basis of their paper and pencil test performance.

What may be a more fruitful approach, at least for certain types of offenders, is a quite different testing procedure. The personality perspective on crime has come full circle, from biological to social to biological again. In the nineteenth century, the influence of the theory of evolution led some to think that criminals represented survival of a more primitive form of human species. Cesare Lombroso, an Italian prison physician, promoted this view by describing prisoners whose skulls exhibited similarities in bumps, ridges, and proportions to those of the apes. This was discredited most effectively by Charles Goring, who showed that the physical features which Lombroso had noted were as frequent in English university students and soldiers as in English convicts. He and others then stressed inherited deficiency of intelligence as the cause of crime, but when tests were refined and amount of schooling held constant, a nearly complete overlap was found in the intelligence test score distributions of criminals and noncriminals.

In the 1920s, the term *psychopath* was increasingly applied to the most persistently criminal individuals. They were described as lacking a conscience. In Illinois prisons a 1933 law required a psychiatric examination of all prisoners, and over 75 percent received the diagnosis *constitutional psychopathic inferior,* implying that they were immoral by heredity. This primarily reflected the psychiatrists' limited experience with people who commit felonies, and their shock in reading the records of criminal behavior. In other prison systems the percentage called psychopath ranged from under 1 percent to 10 percent. The assumption that this trait was inherited was discounted, and the term was so diversely used that its abandonment was widely recommended. In 1952 the *Diagnostic and Statistical Manual, Mental Disorders,* of the American Psychiatric Association replaced the term *psychopath* by *sociopathic personality,* and *sociopath* began to be widely used as a label for persons whom the Manual (1963) describes as "chronically antisocial...always in trouble, profiting neither from experience nor punishment, and maintaining no real loyalties to any person, group or code." The implication was that this trait might be more a product of social experience than of biological inheritance.

The term *psychopath* persists and is often used interchangeably with *sociopath* in clinical psychology and psychiatry. It is still a vague term. The percentage of criminals to whom it is applied varies greatly. Some claim that it is used most readily by those who know their subjects least well, for conscience in dealing with friends is shown by most offenders even when not evident in their predations on strangers.

Nevertheless, a number of studies have found that when persons whose behavior seems to fit most closely the description of a psychopath are compared by certain physiological reaction tests with persons who appear to be most unlike this description, persistent and significant differences are revealed. The psychopaths do not learn to avoid mild electrical shock in psychological learning experiments as quickly as the *normals* learn this.

Also, the heart rates and the electrical resistance of the skin of ostensible psychopaths increase—on the average—more than do those of *normals* following injections of the drug epinephrine, a substance believed to be involved in the brain's reaction to stress (Allen, *et al,* 1969). Such data are interpreted as indicating that psychopaths learn less from physical punishment than others, and do not have reactions to stress as pronounced as those of "normal" people.

Research on what is again called *psychopathy* is being continued on an extensive scale by physiological psychologists with many variations in sampling and measurement procedure. It is clear from the sample selection necessary to find physiological reaction differences that this kind of research will not account for all criminal commitment. Indeed, considerable ability to learn from experience and great role-taking ability is evident in many highly committed professional predatory and illegal-selling criminals for whom the alleged psychopathic physiological reactions would be an occupational handicap. It is certain that these physiological traits do not alone suffice to determine complex behavior such as crime; it is presumed, instead, that they promote criminality more indirectly, by affecting a person's social learning experience, particularly his positive and negative reinforcements from criminal activity and punishment. Questions may also be raised as to whether the demonstrated physiological differences are causes or consequences of a criminal's social experiences, and as to the correlates of these traits when they are found in persons without a record of crime convictions.

Personality traits that are clearly involved in some crime are addictions to various chemical substances. Addiction to a drug, the possession of which is illegal, inherently involves violation of criminal law, and the cost of the drug often motivates property crime, prostitution, or drug-selling to support the addiction. Heavy use of alcohol is, of course, associated with public intoxication and disorderly conduct crimes. It is also found in about half of the known instances of reckless homicide by auto and of rape, most assaults, and a large fraction of forgery. Persons with chronic alcoholism or drug dependence may not be disproportionately committed to criminal rather than to conventional norms apart from those norms violated by their drug possession or intoxicated behavior. The persistence of these addictions, however, means that if these addicts engage in any property or illegal-selling crime to procure funds for purchase of the substances to which they are addicted, there is a high probability of their being extremely persistent in these addiction-supporting crimes.

On the borderline of criminality are some forms of the mental ailment of *paranoia,* characterized by delusions of grandeur or of persecution, or both. Persons with delusions of persecution often are intensely hostile towards certain other persons whom they sometimes endeavor to injure or kill. Their delusions involve systematic reasoning from assumptions about the hated persons which others regard as questionable. They may interpret many insignificant events as confirmations of their assumptions. Legally, a person is not considered to be guilty of a crime if proven insane, but the borderline between the normal and the insane is vague. Therefore, some sensational crimes against persons are interpreted as the results of insanity by many— even when the judicial decision, though perhaps challenged, is that the accused is sane. Paranoia is frequently an aspect of schizophrenia. Theories accounting for it are diverse and controversial. Rates of successful treatment are low. Borderline paranoid schizophrenia and other mental disorders may well be involved in infrequent but dramatic criminality, to be distinguished as *quasi-insane* in our endeavors to typify variations of criminal career.

Chapter 3

TEN POLICY-RELEVANT TYPIFICATIONS OF ADULT CRIME CAREERS

In the previous chapters, crime typologies were examined in the light of the necessary function they perform and the unavoidable limitations which accompany them. Some of the more important variables for typifying careers in crime were also discussed. In this chapter ten categories of criminal career will be described, and social policy in regard to each will be considered. It should be stressed that the classification here is neither exhaustive of all possible differences in crime careers, nor is it uniform with regard to cases within each type. Quite the contrary. Variations within each will be indicated—and it is again stressed that many of the variables by which careers are distinguished are continuous, with every conceivable degree of shading and all the multivariate combinations found in some individuals. Finally, it should be emphasized that no complex human behavior is completely predictable by any description of past behavior. New tension-evoking experiences, new interaction with others, and new communication of an individual with himself may result in the emergence of new behavior, and a redirection of the career by which a criminal has been typed.

Nevertheless, guiding social policy on crime requires that one recognize such patterning as occurs in the tremendous behavior variations of persons defined as criminal, to predict as well as possible the diverse consequences of our policies. The ten criminal career patterns which are distinguished here reflect the crime-descriptive and career-commitment variables discussed in the preceding chapter. It is believed that these types cover the varieties of criminality of most concern for social policy. Methods for preventing or terminating each career pattern will be assessed.

Two contrasting policy strategies are available for reducing crime. One strategy is to cope with individual offenders, the other is to alter the conditions responsible for crime rates. Schur (1969) notes the tendency of our government to "compartmentalize crime" by concentrating its funds on coping with individual criminals when the crime rate might be reduced more effectively if the same funds were expended in altering the conditions conducive to a high crime rate. The latter approach, to invest in prevention of criminality rather than in treatment of criminals, is most appropriate whenever: (a) the number of individual offenders we can deal with is a small fraction of the total; (b) the things we can do by focusing on individuals make negligible impact unless we can alter the societal, community, family, or other conditions with which our subjects must live. Therefore, in this chapter will be discussed policies for changing each type of criminal career as well as policies for preventing them from ever occurring.

Adolescence Recapitulators

Adults who periodically repeat the pattern of delinquency begun in adolescence—or even in childhood—will be referred to here as *adolescence recapitulators.*

As indicated at the beginning of Chapter 2, the period of transition from childhood to adulthood found in our society involves more separation of age groups and a longer duration than ever before. An optimum closeness of generations during this transition period was illustrated by the apprentice of former years who, on first reaching adolescence, began employment with a skilled tradesman for a prescribed number of years. With proper performance he was elevated to journeyman for an additional period, and eventually became a master tradesman. From the beginning of his adolescence he and everyone else knew what his life career would be, and his socialization for it was continuous.

Few adolescents today have this vision of their future, and many of the few with definite vocational orientations change their goals before reaching them. High school and college students commit themselves to a progressively more limited range of alternatives with each passing year, but many are not oriented to specific occupations until midway through college, and some not until long after graduation.

The person whose delinquency in early adolescence results in his leaving school, being expelled, or nominally staying in but conforming only minimally to teacher expectations, experiences the greatest uncertainty in regard to the future (Werthman, 1967). By responding to opportunities for immediate distinction in rebellious peer groups, he falls into a form of what Wiley (1967) called a *mobility trap*—if conformity in school might increase his ultimate status opportunities. Unless he enters the job market at this time he usually drifts into more delinquency. Indeed, school dropouts have a higher delinquency rate before than after leaving school, presumably because many go to work after dropping out (Elliott, 1966). Their responses to psychometric instruments suggest that delinquents view work and crime as equally acceptable alternative means to gain life style goals they share with nondelinquents (Short and Strodtbeck, 1965, Chapter 3). They apparently see themselves as being—and in fact, are—at a crossroads, confronting choices between criminal and noncriminal alternatives, with their decisions a function of the barriers or opportunities they encounter.

As delinquents reach late adolescence, a more definite direction of commitment occurs for many of them. Some get married and settle down into the unskilled or semi-skilled labor force, and some begin to acquire a skill. Getting a girlfriend pregnant and then being obliged to marry her appears to be one of the major means available to a street gang member for withdrawing from commitments to delinquency (Short and Strodtbeck, 1965, Chapter 2). Others drift until caught, alternating periods of disorganized criminality with periods of trying to support themselves at regular jobs.[1] A few become the fulltime occupational predators discussed later; some become drug- or alcohol-addicted, involved in continuous crime to support the addiction.

The bulk of reformatory and much of penitentiary population consists of men in their twenties and thirties struggling in a disorganized fashion towards an adolescent dream of secure manhood. They follow a zig-zag path, alternately "going straight" and settling down at dull and low paying jobs, then, following conflicts with parents or other authority figures, or through disorderly recreational pursuits, becoming involved in crime. This type of offender generally has a mixed criminal record which includes theft of autos for adventure or for flight in crisis, as well as assaults, statutory or quasi-collusive rapes, burglaries, and sometimes robberies. Usually the crimes are not well-planned and the offenders are soon apprehended, although they continue at crime if not apprehended. If they become skillful they may become occupational predators.

These offenders usually operate in pairs, but occasionally in trios or quartets. The persistent "lone wolf" seems to shift into addiction-supporting or vocational predation. In their small primary groups, which often originate in a prison-cell partnership, adolescence recapitulators support

---

[1] As Matza (1969, p. 69) suggests, *drift*, in this context, is episodic anomie or discontinuous normlessness.

each other in delusions of easy gain and escapades. As Asch's (1952) experiments demonstrated, one associate's support of a delusion is often sufficient to elicit another's commitment to it. Peers frequently are the only ones to whom these men have much moral obligation; the stranger, particularly the economically self-sufficient adult, is fair game. The most imaginative and assault-inclined among this offender group are often intrigued with a sense of power that comes from having weapons, and are conspicuous in murder-robbery crimes. Irwin's "Disorganized Criminal" exemplifies this type well, as do most of his "State-Raised Youth" (1970). They are also illustrated in Glaser's cases of "Early Reformation after Extensive Crime," and in the less professionally criminal of his "Eventual Recidivists" (1969).

The adolescence recapitulator usually has had strains in his relationship with his parents as cause or consequence of his delinquency. Often one or both parents were unavailable, unstable, or even adolescence recapitulators themselves. Statistical research has shown (Glaser, 1969, Chapter 14), that during imprisonment "absence makes the heart grow fonder" in the inmate's relationships with parents, while ties with friends and with spouses follow the maxim, "out of sight, out of mind." Although these offenders repeatedly leave home in conflict, they are usually welcomed back to the parental home when "down and out." All assure each other that things will now go well, but conflict recurs and they leave or are ejected again. Usually the essence of the conflict is the offspring's desire to be his own boss with respect to the hours he keeps, his associates, and his work patterns, and the ensuing resentment at parental efforts to control these.

The adolescence recapitulator chafes for a sense of manhood, and tries to achieve it in his recreation pattern. Starting with little money and few skills on release from an institution, he cannot quickly gain independence, and the costs of his recreation in money, time, and fatigue create strains at his home and job. A high rate of turnover in employment is typical, with much of the job loss reflecting conflicts with authority figures on the job similar to those he had with his parents. From interviews with over 300 returned federal parole violators (Glaser, 1969), it was evident that most of the men in their twenties and thirties who had been incarcerated two to five times as juveniles and adults repeated at each release approximately the same sequence of finding havens at home and then getting into difficulties with the law in their impatience to achieve independence from their homes.

The solution for this type of criminal career problem must be multifaceted. Optimum prevention could be achieved if their early delinquency and school conflicts were diminished by the reduction of their isolation from the conventional world through small programs of on-the-job training, or through programmed education within larger schools not solely for problem youth. Assignment to such alternative schooling patterns, staffed by auxiliary school personnel from the community, is preferable to the practice of suspending and ejecting a youth whenever he "acts up" in school, thus increasing both his academic handicaps and his commitment to delinquency.

For those who are incarcerated because of repeated serious offenses, creating incentives to employment and intensive education—primarily by paying for lessons mastered in the institution—has made possible several years of schooling recuperation in one year (McKee, 1968; Cohen, et al, 1966). This may all be lost if the prisoner is again released with no funds to the home situation where the previous difficulties occurred.

In our largest cities, small centers for graduated release from prison have proven especially effective in reducing the recidivism rates of the adolescence recapitulator. In these institutions, pioneered by the federal prison system, twenty or thirty men spend the last three or four months of their prison term in part of a large hotel or other residential structure in the center of the city to which they will be released. They leave these centers daily to seek jobs or to work when they have obtained jobs, returning to the center at night. Counseling is focused on discussing their experiences of each day, and their anticipations for the following day. Gradually they are given longer passes for evening or weekend recreation, and to visit their prospective homes. Great emphasis is placed on budgeting. At first they receive pocket money but when they start earning they pay most of their own expenses, and are required to open a savings account for everything above a certain minimum.

At the time they begin their parole, these men—though technically they have been prisoners—usually have a longer work record and more savings than they ever had previously. Often they go through three or four jobs in the first month, but most of them gradually achieve the ability to hold a job. When those released after such a program were compared with similar prisoners released before the programs existed, it was found that the greatest reduction in recidivism occurred for the highest failure rate categories (Hall, et al, 1966). These were the recidivist auto thieves who were in federal prisons because they drove stolen autos across state lines; they exemplify the adolescent flight-for-independence pattern continued into young adulthood.

The problems of the adolescence recapitulator are shared by an increasing proportion of young adults, though most do not become involved in major predations. A reduction of the generation gap through involvement of more youth in organized adult activities, and more adults in youth activities—centering particularly in the schools, but with more structuring of many alternative study and employment opportunities—would seem to be the best way to cope with many types of problems arising in youth's efforts at transition to a self-sufficient adulthood.

Subcultural Assaulters

Persons who live in a subculture emphasizing violence as a value more than does the rest of our society are referred to here as *subcultural assaulters*. They physically attack others because this is what is expected in their social circle when one is severely affronted, or one's manliness is challenged.

Violent crime is the most disturbing to the public, who often think of it as just the result of a sick mind, hence a purely psychological problem. That this is not an adequate explanation is suggested by the fact that violence is disproportionately concentrated in certain cultural groups.

The most extreme form of assault is murder, but all non-negligent homicide is highly correlated with nonlethal assault, for most murders appear to be committed in the heat of anger, with the murderer grabbing whatever weapon happens to be at hand. Chance availability of the weapon or a chance way in which the body falls often determines whether the assault is deadly. The highly calculated schemes portrayed in murder films or mystery stories illustrate types of murder that are much more infrequent and do not concern us in this section. The discrepancy between reality and the popular conception of murder is highlighted by analyses finding that 26 percent of murders in Philadelphia and 38 percent of those in Chicago were victim-precipitated—that is, the person killed struck the first blow in the altercation which led to his demise (Wolfgang, 1958; Voss and Hepburn, 1968).

We cannot precisely know the prevalence of assault because it is so often not reported to the police and is inconsistently recorded when reported. Homicide is the offense on which our statistics on total rates are most complete. These data are compiled not only by police departments, but also by departments of public health, who tabulate statistics on the causes of death from physicians' death certificates. In recent years rates from these two independent sources have been close to identical, inspiring confidence that both are highly accurate.

Because most murders are the outcome of assaults, we can assume that the distribution and trend in assault is roughly parallel with that in murder. That assault and murder have similar correlates in terms of time of occurrence, location, relationship between offender and victim, and other features was demonstrated by Pittman and Handy (1964). The homicide rate fluctuates not only with the assault rate, however, but also with the proportion of assaults that employ a lethal weapon, particularly a handgun. This proportion varies with the prevalence of such weapons in the population, as will be discussed later.

A striking fact regarding murder in the United States is that it used to be more frequent than it is now. In 1933 the United States had 9.7

deaths by non-negligent homicide per 100,000 people. This declined to 4.5 per 100,000 in 1955, but it rose in the 1960s, reaching 7.2 in 1969. In Boston, the largest American city for which good records covering more than a century have been found and tabulated, it is evident that the murder rate was about twice as high in the nineteenth as in the twentieth century (Ferdinand, 1967).

The frequency of homicide varies greatly from one nation to the next and among the states of our country. The highest rates are found in Latin America, where Colombia and Mexico have reported over thirty murders per 100,000 persons per year. On the other hand, northwestern European countries have far lower rates than the United States—the British, Danish, and Norwegians each reporting about one per 200,000 people per year, the Dutch one per 300,000, and the Irish (Eire) one per half-million (Wolfgang and Ferracuti, 1967, pp. 274–275).

Within the United States, murder is most frequent in the Southeast; the highest state rates reported by the F.B.I. for 1969 were 13.7 per 100,000 in Alabama and 12.5 in South Carolina. The lowest state rate was North Dakota's 0.2 per 100,000, next was Iowa with 1.4, Maine was third with 1.6, and Minnesota fourth with 1.9; the lowest rate for a major region, however, was 3.0 for New England compared with 4.5 for the west north-central states which are the next lowest.

Homicide rates are generally highest in low status components of the population. Formerly they were higher in rural than in urban areas of the United States, but the reverse has been true since mid-century. A possible reason is that until the mechanization of agriculture accelerated in the post-World War II years, rural areas had more of the poor people with unstable livelihoods, the groups to which subcultures of violence appear to be most compatible. Our *subcultural assaulters* are closest to the *lower class "man"* in Irwin's (1970) types. The peak age for murder is the twenties, an age of economic and social status insecurity.

In the United States, females are the victims in almost one-fourth the murders, and the killers in one-eighth of them, reflecting the present differences in sex role in our society, and the fact that insecurity in love as well as in economics appreciably affects the murder rate. Murders by females, however, are also highest in povertous groups with subcultures of violence where males have high assault and homicide rates. There appears to be some validity to the maxim, "When the wolf's at the door, love flies out the window." In England, a third of the homicides are followed by the suicide of the murderer, but in the United States this occurs in less than 5 percent of the cases. These data suggest that more of the murders in the United States express subcultures of violence rather than deep-seated personality conflicts.

Homicide is most frequent in areas where violence is the expected behavior, considered morally obligatory in response to verbal insults or rebuffs. Latin American countries are noted for concern of males with *machismo* or manliness, to which tremendous value is attached; male "honor" is defended by physical violence. The highest national rates of all, those for Colombia, are associated with political feuds and with robberies, in addition to the *machismo* values.

Most murder occurs in leisure gatherings, among friends or relatives, which explains why its peak season is the summer, with December—the holiday month—highest for the rest of the year. This also explains why it occurs most frequently in the evenings and on weekends. Alcohol is present in both the offender and the victim in over half the murder cases.

Two-thirds of the female murder victims and half the males are killed in the home, which suggests that home is the most dangerous place to be— although commercial drinking and recreation places are also frequent murder settings. The Chicago study (Voss and Hepburn, 1968) reports that in about half the cases the relationship between the murderer and victim is that of close friend or relative, casual acquaintances account for less than a third of all murder cases, and only about a fifth are strangers, with robbery the motive in most of the latter. In about a fifth of the cases the murderer and victim were married to each other.

Persons who are educated are much less likely to commit murder than those who are not. Presumably, education teaches verbal alternatives to physical violence, or at any rate "snide remarks" and snubs are more the norms for aggression among the educated than physical assault. The long-run decline in the United States murder rate may have been mainly a product of more prevalent education plus increased economic security.

In the United States, the children of poverty-stricken immigrants have usually had the highest rates of assaultive crime (with the exception of those in several ethnic groups, such as the Chinese and Jews, where the family and ethnic community were able to inculcate anti-violence values). Thus, in the 1920s and 1930s the highest rates of violent crime in northern cities were found in young adults of Polish and Italian descent. In recent years the murder rate of Blacks has been over twice that of Whites, but the rates for each group have the same correlates, which suggests that they have the same causes. Within both racial groups, murder rates have been highest in the South and among the poorest and least educated. But the Blacks are more concentrated in the South, and generally poorer and less educated than Whites. It has been demonstrated that one can predict rather accurately Black murder rates from the murder rates of Whites in the states from which the Blacks come (Pettigrew and Spier, 1962). Incidentally, murderer and victim are of the same race in about 95 percent of the cases.

The increase in homicide rates since 1958 appears to have had three main causes. Since the end of World War II there has been a large migration of population from areas which previously had the most intense subculture of violence—to city slums from the rural South, and to western cities from Mexico. The younger migrants and the children of migrants, who were reared in the slums, had less extended family and neighborhood assistance than prevailed in the migrants' former communities, and experienced greater problems. Thus the previously higher rural murder rates were perhaps exceeded by city rates in the 1950s as a result of rural-to-urban migration, and as a result of stresses of city life on the offspring of migrants reared in slum conditions of high tension and weak adult controls.

A second cause of increased murder rates is simply the population trend. The proportion of United States population in their twenties, the peak age range for murder, achieved a new high during the late 1960s, a reflection of the post-World War II baby boom.

A third cause for the larger number of murders is the possession of firearms by more people following the urban riots of the 1960s. The sale of handguns quadrupled from 1962 to 1968 and the sale of long guns doubled (Newton and Zimring, 1969). The percentage of homicides caused by firearms has increased steadily each year from 53 percent in 1961 to 65 percent in 1968, with 50 percent due to handguns. Knives or other cutting instruments accounted for 19 percent, blows or strangulation without weapons 8 percent, and other methods (clubs, poisons, drownings, etc.) 8 percent.

Assault is often repeated when it has no unpleasant consequences for the assaulter. Arrest for simple assault usually results in a minor jail term. There is some reason to believe that fines may be as effective a deterrent as jail. A common device is to require the assaulter to post several hundred dollars as a peace bond, which he forfeits should he again molest the victim. Unfortunately, no statistical analyses or controled experiments have been made for rigorous assessment of these deterrence methods.

Our penalties for murderers are almost invariably effective in preventing repetition. Formerly, they were executed, but the use of the death penalty has declined, perhaps in part because of evidence that variation in its use had no effect on the homicide rate (Sellin, 1967, pp. 135–160). Today most murderers are given long prison terms, usually designated life, although most are eligible for parole in fifteen to twenty-five years. The parole violation rate for murderers is the lowest of any offense, and less than 1 percent of those released repeat this crime. (Age at release is doubtless a factor in this.)

For several decades three murder statistics distinguished the southern states: the most frequent use of the death penalty, the shortest prison terms for those murderers who escaped execution, and the highest murder rates. This suggests that the highest degree of tolerance for murder occurs where subcultures of violence prevail. High use of the death penalty as well as short prison sentences for murder were also reported in Latin American countries where murder rates are high. In the 1960s executions gradually ceased in the United States, perhaps reflecting a change in cultural valuation of violence as well as the irrelevance of executions to murder rates.

One cannot eliminate altercations, but one might make them less deadly by reducing the prevalence of firearms. Opponents of firearms control cite the Second Amendment to the United States Constitution, which asserts: "A well regulated militia, being necessary to the security of a free State, the right of the people to keep and bear arms shall not be infringed." Here "militia" refers only to citizens enrolled and drilled in a state military organization other than the regular armed forces, which today means the National Guard. Courts have upheld laws that impose severe penalties for unlicensed possession of handguns, deny gun licenses to persons with a criminal record, and require advance registration and approval of transfers of ownership. In the northeastern states, where the laws have long been most strict, 46 percent of the murders result from firearms; in the South, where they are least strict, guns account for 73 percent. In the north central states 70 percent of murders are caused by firearms, and in the West 61 percent. In Detroit, where handgun owners are registered under state law but licenses are not greatly restricted, the number of homicides by gun increased year-by-year in 1965–1968, almost in direct proportion to the fourfold increase in gun owners during this period (Newton and Zimring, 1969, pp. 69–74). Nevertheless, strong lobbies fight gun control, national laws remain quite weak, and state laws are extremely diverse. (See Newton and Zimring, 1969 for legislative facts and arguments.)

The fact that gross rates of violence reflect subcultural conditions does not eliminate personality as a factor in violence. Within each subculturally different group some individuals are of more volatile temper and some physically express their feelings more readily (see Toch, 1969, pp. 189–195). Some of the personality factors superimposed on subcultural values will be dealt with in discussing our *quasi-insane assaulter* type. The great contrasts in overall rates from one area or subgroup to another over a period of time suggest that most of the variance in assault and homicide rates reflects cultural values associated with educational and economic deprivation. It follows that the most effective means of reducing assault and homicide is to upgrade the education of the educationally deprived, and to reduce the extent of their insecurity in employment and status. This could conceivably be achieved by massive and imaginative programs, some already initiated on a small scale. A by-product of such education and employment advancement should be a renewed decline in the United States assault and homicide rates, such as the decline which occurred following the peaking of these rates during the Great Depression of the early 1930s.

Addiction-Supporting Predators

Persons who commit property crimes primarily to procure funds for the purchase of some mood-altering drug are referred to here as *addiction-supporting predators*. In the United States, alcohol is the drug to which addiction most frequently occurs. It is estimated that at least two-thirds of American adults use alcoholic beverages, and the number classified as *chronic alcoholics* or *heavy drinkers* ranges from four to seven million, depending on how these terms are defined (Blum and Braunstein, 1967). Figures on opiate use are even more uncertain, but it is frequently estimated that one can double the sixty thousand addicts officially reported by the Federal Bureau of Narcotics. A late 1969 Gallup poll found 4 percent of the United States adult population had used marijuana—12 percent of the population from twenty to twenty-nine years old. A December 1970 Gallup poll found 42 percent of college students had tried marijuana. The estimates for barbiturates, amphetamines, and other drugs are more speculative.

The term *addiction* is used here in its increasingly prevalent meaning as any compulsive and persistent use or habituation. A narrower conception, sometimes preferred, makes *addiction* clearly applicable to only the opiates and barbiturates among common drugs, for it refers to the presence of two physiological phenomena: (1) *tolerance,* identified by the body's need for an increasingly higher dose to feel the effects of the drug (usually reaching an upper limit, but at a dosage dangerous to non-users); (2) *withdrawal syndrome,* after tolerance is developed, identified by acute illness symptoms if intake of the drug abruptly terminates. The extreme craving for drugs characteristic of heroin addicts reflects the fact that they feel approximately normal when their bodies contain a high concentration of opiates, but when the drug in their bodies diminishes they feel the onset of extreme illness (nausea, cramps, chills, etc.), and know that more opiate intake will give dramatic relief. Cross-tolerance exists among various opium-derived and synthetic opiate drugs, so one can be substituted for another.

The use of marijuana, amphetamines, and LSD is usually reported to be not associated with an extreme compulsion, so desperate behavior to procure more of such drugs is not as characteristic of their use as it is of alcohol, opiates, and barbiturates. Most users of the less addictive drugs shift to another substance when their supply of one runs out.

There is no clear consensus among scientists as to the causes of alcoholism. It is widely distributed in society, although less frequent in ethnic groups which usually drink wines with special meals, than in those for whom distilled beverages of higher alcoholic content (whiskies, brandies, vodka, gin, etc.) are customary. A reasonable—though tentative—conclusion from the scientific literature is that most alcoholics are persons highly dependent on primary group relationships, that drinking is initially done largely for the uninhibited fellowship and intimacy associated with being drunk together, that it is more avidly pursued by persons with strains in their regular primary group relationships, and finally, that a conditioning process creates the later compulsive and even lone heavy drinking of the chronic alcoholic. Individual psychotherapy—from aversive conditioning with chemicals that create nausea when one drinks alcoholic beverages, to psychoanalysis—demonstrates only a small percentage of long-run cures. All treatment programs are highly affected by the extent of the alcoholic's motivation to change which, if persistent, may suffice in itself. Most terminations of both alcoholism and drug addiction are not abruptly achieved, but come after a cycle of gradually longer abstinence periods and briefer relapses.

The monetary cost of drink for an alcoholic is not extreme; most can be satiated with four to six dollars worth of the cheaper bottled beverages per day or several times this expenditure for drinks at bars. Many chronic alcoholics support their habit legitimately. The incompatibility of extreme alcoholism with regular employment or with meeting other financial obligations creates some economic desperation, but those who commit property predations in order to keep drinking are usually involved in only petty and sporadic offenses. As indicated earlier, the crime distinctly associated with alcoholism is naïve check forgery.

Frequently the checks are on the accounts of relatives or are cashed with someone the drinker knows so they are readily traced. Most of the checks do not result in prosecution because of the victim's relationship to the forger, the small amount involved, and the fact that when the check bounces, he makes or promises to make restitution. Eventually, however, people lose patience, as the compulsion to drink results in continual repetition of this offense.

Lobbying by commercial interests in many states has resulted in severe prison sentences for even small check forgeries, although they are rarely imposed on offenders who are not persistent. When one encounters a forger in a state prison he is usually an alcoholic and a recidivist forger, and he has one of the highest parole failure probabilities because of the prospect of his return to drinking and forgery.

The pattern of opiate use in the United States has shifted markedly. Morphine was an unregulated and widely-used pain reliever after its discovery early in the nineteenth century. Armies of both sides in the Civil War distributed it to wounded soldiers for self-administration, and it was common in mining areas because of injuries and silicosis. The opiate laudanum was frequently used by older people for the aches and pains of age, and by women for discomforts of the menstrual cycle and menopause. In conjunction with the Prohibition movement against alcoholic beverages, however, lurid tales of "dope fiends" were promulgated early in the twentieth century, and in 1914 the Harrison Act was passed, restricting distribution of opiates to licensed medical channels. Its manner of enforcement, however, also discouraged some medical usage (Lindesmith, 1965, pp. 3–98).

A survey of addicts committed to the United States Public Health Hospital in Lexington during the 1930s revealed that most were middle-aged, white, and from the rural South. During World War II the supply of morphine was restricted by the needs of the armed forces and the difficulties of importing opium from the Middle and Far East. It was apparently in this period that heroin distribution became an especially profitable field of organized illegal selling, and was exploited by criminal groups based in the slums. They evidently extended their market by sales promotions in their home communities, for addiction shifted location dramatically during the 1940s. It became predominantly characteristic of young adults of minority groups in the largest American cities, particularly New York (Ball, 1965).

An addict's opiate expense varies from fifteen or twenty to well over one hundred dollars per day, with the average near the lower figures. This refers exclusively to the so-called *street addict*, the person who procures his drugs primarily through illegal peddlers dealing mainly in heroin. An additional economic strain involved in street opiate addiction is the fact that it impedes employment for most, especially when heroin is used. When this opiate is injected into a vein, it narcotizes more rapidly than other drugs, hence is more disabling. It is also metabolized more rapidly, and therefore must be replenished sooner, to avoid withdrawal symptoms. There are also addicts among physicians, pharmacists, and nurses who divert morphine or other opiates from medical channels at little or no cost to themselves.

The pre-World War II addicts who engaged in crime usually did so after becoming addicted and many violated no laws except those on the possession of opiates. Today's addicts are more often delinquent or criminal before becoming addicted and thereafter support their habit by more persistent crime (O'Donnell, 1966). The most frequent offenses among male addicts are theft and burglary, while the 10 to 20 percent who are female support themselves predominantly by prostitution, often with an addict pimp. A large proportion peddle drugs at times, usually in conjunction with purchasing at a lower price by buying enough for themselves and others, and still others get drugs as a rental fee for cookers and syringes. The pressure to keep continually resupplied with the drug, and to steal and sell goods to get money to do this creates an exhausting round of activity most inappropriately labeled *retreatism;* it is more accurately described by the addicts' term for all their money-seeking efforts—*hustling.* (See Lewis, 1970 for an apt comparison of the hustler's values with those of a legitimate businessman.)

Change in the demographic distribution of opiate addiction suggests some change in its causation, although many psychologists believe that hyper-dependent *addiction-prone* personalities still predominate among both opiate addicts and alcoholics. As indicated, addicts formerly were mostly middle-aged or older and equally male and female. Their use of these drugs was related to medical complaints. Although such addicts still exist, the initiation of drug use by today's predominantly young minority group and ex-delinquent addicts in large-city slums has been explained by what could be called a *relative deprivation-differential anticipation* theory. Diverse evidence indicates that they are typically young persons blocked from achieving conventional aspirations by their early involvement in delinquency (much as the adolescence recapitulators are) and attracted to drug circles by the sense of esoteric achievement and accomplishment available from being connoisseurs of drug consumption and experts at the "hustle" (Finestone, 1957; Abrams, *et al,* 1968; Glaser, *et al,* 1971).

Social policies to cope with opiate addiction have been extremely ineffective until recently. During the 1950s penalties for possession were made increasingly severe, then stabilized with a 1956 federal law whose provisions included: two to five years imprisonment on the first narcotics possession offense, but probation permissible; five to twenty years imprisonment on the second possession or first selling offense, with probation or parole forbidden. For sale of heroin by a person over eighteen to a person under eighteen, however, the penalty is ten years to life without probation or parole, or a death sentence if recommended by a jury. Over forty states in the 1950s enacted Uniform Narcotic Drug Acts, based on a model prepared by the U.S. Bureau of Narcotics, with penalties similar to or more severe than the federal statute. They defined "narcotics" under these laws as comprising either marijuana or any of the opiates.

In many areas such penalties are more honored in the breach than in fulfilment, especially when marijuana is involved. A newspaper's follow-up of over 100 marijuana arrests in Champaign-Urbana, Illinois in the 1960s found none had received a conviction for narcotics possession under the Uniform Act, and most had all charges dismissed. On repeated heroin possession, Chicago courts accepted pleas of guilty to a first possession charge, and imposed the two- to five-year sentence, ignoring the mandatory five- to twenty-year legislation. In areas where drug offenses are infrequent, however, penalties are more often those specified by law, particularly when the offender is a stranger. If drug law violations are charged in conjunction with predations, penalties are more severe. Informal norms develop in courts as to which types of persons deserve which types of punishment regardless of formal charges (Sudnow, 1965). When a college or high school student with no criminal record possesses marijuana there is reluctance to punish him more severely than the court generally punishes recidivist predators. Furthermore, police procedure in arresting or in seizing evidence is frequently open to legal challenge, and defense lawyers can obtain dismissal on technical grounds or persuade the prosecutor to accept a plea of guilty on lesser charges, thus giving the prosecutor a politically attractive record of convicting a higher percentage of accused persons.

Regardless of punishment, drug use appears to have increased in the later 1960s, and reached a younger group. The drugs are so compact and their use so widely dispersed that risk of apprehension for sale or possession is small, and profits of sales are immense. Careful estimates of New York City drug use distribution were made in 1969 by correcting total number of addicts listed in police or hospital records for each neighborhood by a multiplier based on the percent of those found dead from drugs who were not listed in these records (one of several indices of completeness of the records). The estimate indicated that 2 percent of the population of ages sixteen to forty-five in New York City were regular users of opiates, and in one slum area the percentage reached nearly 15 (Koval, 1969). One can almost double these rates if males alone are considered, since they constitute about half the population but over 80 percent of the addicts. Police estimates of the proportion of theft and burglary in New York to support heroin addiction ranged from one-third to one-half, and most of the prostitutes were said to be addicts. Furthermore, those incarcerated for drug offenses usually relapsed to drug use soon after release, even when confined long enough to have completely recovered from withdrawal symptoms. It was estimated that since half the nation's opiate addicts were in New York City the problem was less acute elsewhere, but it was still disturbing in all large cities. Marijuana and other nonopiate drugs were more widely dispersed nationally.

Failure of purely punitive measures led to a medical approach. The federal government established hospitals, first at Lexington and later at Fort Worth, for the voluntary confinement of addicts desiring treatment, and for the treatment of addicted federal prison inmates. Follow-up studies of Lexington patients indicated relapse of over 90 percent for those from New York City in post-World War II years, but a tapering off of drug use with age, hence with duration of the follow-up period (O'Donnell, 1965). In 1962 the Supreme Court in *Robinson* v. *California* voided that state's penalties for addiction, construing it as a status rather than an offense, but suggesting that hospitals for civil commitment of addicts be established, as for the mentally ill. The establishment of such hospitals had already begun, but their number was expanded immediately in California, where a part of the prison system was redesignated a "Rehabilitation Center"— though still administered by the Department of Corrections. New York followed in 1967, but with a separate agency, and predominantly nonprison structures and staff. New York also subsidized a large variety of voluntary treatment agencies.

An extremely influential treatment model was initiated in 1935 when a physician and a stockbroker met by chance, discovered they benefitted from telling one another about their problems with alcoholism, and founded Alcoholics Anonymous. The commitments of this group are to admit to themselves and others that they have been unable to control their alcoholism, to seek help from one another and from "a Power greater than ourselves," to confess their wrongs, to make restitution to those they have hurt, and to try to help other alcoholics. One expert asserts: "It is probable that more contemporary alcoholics have found sobriety through the fellowship of Alcoholics Anonymous than through all other agencies combined" (Maxwell, 1962). They meet in small groups, the intimacy of which perhaps provides some of the fellowship they sought in drinking. Their continually helping other alcoholics plus their belief in their abnormal susceptibility to alcoholism may commit them to abstinence. It should be noted that Alcoholics Anonymous cannot get most alcoholics to participate, nor all that do to persist without occasional relapse.

Analogous organizations for opiate addicts began in 1959 when an Alcoholics Anonymous member founded Synanon for ex-addicts, in California. It now has branches in several parts of the United States and has been copied by scores of other ex-addict groups. They differ from Alcoholics Anonymous in having vehement verbal exchanges to break down the rationalizations of the addicts rather than genteel discussions (Yablonsky, 1964). Synanon and most of its imitators are primarily residential centers and are partly self-sufficient through various business enterprises in which the ex-addicts are employed. Their severe discipline and persistent verbal aggression is mixed with close primary group affection and mutual aid. There are many ex-addicts to attest to the effectiveness of this treatment method, but precise evaluation is impossible because intake is highly selective (necessarily limited to those volunteers who are acceptable to the group), an appreciable number who leave or are ejected are not counted as treated, and follow-up data are not collected systematically on all former participants. It is clear that those who remain in these groups do not use drugs, and group membership, including fulltime residence, may last an indefinite number of years.

Another dramatic treatment for addiction resembles the programs of Britain and other countries, where drugs are supplied legally to addicts under medical supervision. In the United States such legalization has been restricted to methadone—a synthetic opiate developed by the Germans as a substitute for morphine during World War II, and first used in the United States for relief of withdrawal symptoms—in dosages gradually tapered down to zero. Methadone taken orally prevents withdrawal symptoms for twenty-four to forty-eight hours (a new type—acetylmethadol—lasts about twice as long), and does not impede employment as much as the more quickly metabolized heroin.

Under "Methadone Maintenance Treatment," developed in the mid-1960s by Doctors Vincent P. Dole and Marie Nyswander of Rockefeller University, instead of diminishing the daily methadone dosage it is increased until it is sufficiently high to prevent the addict from feeling any effect from additional opiates. When used in conjunction with counseling and other assistance, methadone maintenance has consistently had a success rate of 70 to 80 percent measured in terms of cessation of criminality and the eventual resumption of regular employment (Dole, *et al,* 1968). Contrastingly, civil commitment patients appear to have a relapse rate of well over 80 percent (Kramer and Bass, 1969). The cost of methadone is only fifteen or twenty cents per day, and its use in treatment is growing rapidly. The British now encourage their addicts to switch from injecting heroin or morphine to taking methadone. Although the Dole-Nyswander approach anticipates that addicts must continue to take methadone for the rest of their lives—just as diabetics must take insulin—the Illinois Drug Abuse Project under Dr. Jerry Jaffe of the University of Chicago utilizes group relationships among addicts on methadone somewhat in the Synanon mode, and the members strive to achieve a target of complete abstinence in less than two years. An appreciable number diminish and even terminate dosage within a year without relapsing to heroin. The opportunity to resume methadone is kept open for them, however, as a "safety valve" alternative (Jaffe, *et al,* 1969).

If the relative deprivation-differential anticipation explanation for addiction in today's slum youth is correct, the preventive remedies of diversified education and employment facilitation proposed for the adolescence recapitulators and the subcultural assaulters would also reduce youthful addiction. In any case, a purely punitive approach to drug addiction has clearly proven futile. If psychotherapy and mutual aid groups of ex-addicts are available for those who seek them, and if methadone is available for other addicts, the addict's current need to engage in predation or prostitution will diminish. This realization is being reached by more and more people involved in social policy formation, but there is still considerable clinging to the demonstrably less effective approach of incarceration.

Historically, social reaction to consumption which many find disturbing seems to have involved a shifting from complete permissiveness to complete prohibition, then lacking the ability to enforce the prohibition, to some type of regulation. In the case of alcoholic beverages this cycle occurred in the repeal of Prohibition, followed by regulations regarding the age of persons to whom drink may be sold, the location and character of sellers, the sale of alcoholic beverages to persons already intoxicated, and drunken driving. It appears that a system is evolving which encompasses some type of licensed distribution of synthetic opiates of the methadone type to persons already addicted and in an approved treatment program, but it may be too early to discern the exact form it will take.

Vocational Predators

Persons who support themselves for many years primarily by unlawfully taking money or property from others are referred to here as *vocational predators.*

The line between vocational and other types of predation is not always clear. Adolescence recapitulators who succeed in predations often repeat them until they are caught. They think of themselves as professionals in crime, but they tend to be unskilled to begin with, and to become increasingly reckless with each offense, so they are soon caught. Upon release they do not usually revert to crime immediately. The addiction-supporting predators, especially opiate addicts, frequently become vocational predators—they support themselves and their addiction entirely by property crimes. That most are not highly committed to it as a vocation, however, is suggested by the fact that when they "kick the drug habit," few persist in vocational crime.

Vocational predators can be usefully divided by the percentage of time in which they operate alone rather than in groups. Whatever is technically most efficient for their criminal specialty generally determines this. If they collaborate with others in their vocation—committing crimes as teams, disposing of stolen goods, or merely socializing extensively with other offenders—they collectively develop and share an occupational subculture. Subcultures are found in all occupations, criminal and legitimate, in which participants have a sense of fraternity, pride, and esoteric skills or knowledge. They usually develop some language familiar only to the initiated, share common standards in appraising each other's qualifications, and have a variety of distinctive customs and traditions, whether they are railroad men, plumbers, butchers or thieves.

Because people who make a vocation of crime are especially cautious, they are not caught as readily as amateurs, and their criminal subcultures are not known by many. Consequently, we do not have extensive information on them. A few studies, however, have revealed much about some property crime specialties. For example, David Maurer, a professor of English at the University of Louisville who specializes in the philology of criminal argot, has become perhaps our leading informant on confidence game and pickpocket subcultures (1940, 1964).

The confidence man or "bunco artist" is essentially a person who exploits and exaggerates our societal value of "getting rich quick" by "one's wits." He artfully convinces a victim of his access to "inside dope" on a fabulous investment opportunity, sometimes an illegal one, that will yield high returns. The victim is then enticed into making larger investments by being given high returns quickly on his first payments. Eventually, of course, the confidence man disappears with a large sum of investment money, although one of his most effective ploys is to convince the investor that something went wrong so that it is a legitimate loss. Frequently, the victim does not even report his loss to the police, because he does not realize he was cheated, because he is ashamed to admit being duped, or because he thinks he was guilty of criminal activity in the investments made for him.

Confidence men usually work in teams of two or more. One will strike up an acquaintance with the victim, known as the "mark," and gain his confidence. A profitable "mark" is often a self-made businessman especially accessible to strangers when away from home and proud of his affluence as evidence of his astuteness. The confidence man pretends that he is even more affluent, but that he respects the mark as a good business-man. He offers the "mark" a great business opportunity which requires a meeting with one or more other businessmen who are actually confederates in the confidence game. Once rapport is developed, this drama of deception may be maintained for a considerable period, even after the "mark" returns to his home community, to impress upon him the high returns on small investments—until his greed lures him into a large investment.

It is no accident that the confidence man is often referred to col-loquially as a "con artist," for he is a consummate actor. His usually high intelligence and thespian talents make him a colorful personality, highly convincing in his projected roles. An astute psychologist, his portrayals are tailored to what he perceives as the mark's particular vanity. Above all, he is the great drummer, the smooth super-salesman, who could be successful in the legitimate world if he were concerned for others and willing to work under acceptable rules. The operations of unethical used-car salesmen and of purveyors of medical quackery border on or sometimes are confidence games.

Unfortunately, there is seldom a Robin Hood role in the con artist's vast repertoire. Opportunity determines his victims and he preys remorse-lessly upon the relatively poor as well as the "well heeled." The variety of frauds are amazing. Some are so simple that it is surprising that anyone can be duped, but they recur regularly. The following, for example, is an actual account of the standard confidence game known as "pigeon drop," as described in the Champaign-Urbana, Illinois *Courier:*

> Mrs._____was approached in the_____National Bank by two women who feigned an acquaintanceship with her and then reported finding a wallet containing $200.
> The three were to split the contents but one of the women first went to consult "her boss," and then reported there actually was $1,700.
> Mrs._____was required to produce $500 to prove that she was "used to money" before the split.
> She cashed a check for $500 in the bank and turned over the money to the women, but before getting her "share" was instructed to consult their "boss" at a non-existent address.

   When Mrs._____returned from her futile trip the two women
had vanished.[2]

It is often difficult to make a clear distinction between confidence
games and certain activities considered legitimate business—misrepresentation in selling or in offering credit terms, pushing unnecessary repair service
on automobiles, television sets, furnaces, and other devices, or charging for
services not performed. These activities are against the law, but the law
is not enforced and any effort to enforce it raises objections to interference
with free enterprise. The confidence man is, in a sense, a person who takes
advantage of free enterprise values by extending the rule "let the buyer
beware" beyond the normal tolerance level.

Another type of vocational predator is the pickpocket. These specialists
work around crowds, usually as a team of two or three. One may pretend
to bump accidentally into the victim, and then be very apologetic or otherwise divert his attention, while the second one picks his pocket. They practice extensively and are extremely adept in removing a billfold without the
victim's awareness. Frequently a third accomplice takes the stolen money
and immediately leaves the area so that the wallet is not found on anyone
the victim could suspect, should he discover his loss.

Professional predators who work in teams refine their skills to a high
degree and are excellent actors. They are careful whom they recruit, and
a novice must go through a long apprenticeship. Some are married and
have families. Sometimes the spouse is misinformed as to her husband's
employment, but sometimes she knows about it or is even a confederate.

Professional bank robbery and safecracking teams are few in number,
but are prestigeful among criminals because they take great risks for high
stakes. Burglary remains a major professional category. Those who enter
houses or apartments frequently operate alone, while those plying business
establishments act as a team and load merchandise into trucks. In either case
they must maintain relationships with dealers in stolen goods (an illegal
selling profession). Burglaries are often performed to fill orders for a specific
type of product for which the dealer has already made a selling arrangement.
Thieves who prey on parked trucks or freight cars, and robbers who high-
jack vehicles at gunpoint are also involved in regular relationships with
dealers.

Some lone vocational predators start with naïve and avocational crime,
but drop other types of employment when they experience success in crime.
Professional "boosters" are of this type, engaging regularly in shoplifting,
selling primarily to second-hand shops or used clothing dealers (Cameron,
1964). Systematic check forgers are a similar type (Lemert, 1967, Chapters
8 and 9). Although they generally work alone, they occasionally operate

[2] Reprinted with permission of the *Champaign-Urbana Courier.*

in pairs or trios. The "booster" activity, for instance, may include a lookout to warn when a store employee is watching, or to divert him.

Another noteworthy vocational predator is the professional killer. While this occupation accounts for a small percent of the total murders in the United States, the police practically never solve them. Prominent among offenses ascribed to these professionals is the killing of witnesses against persons being prosecuted for organized illegal selling, and the assassination of competitive leaders in such selling. In Chicago, where over 90 percent of the total murders had been cleared by arrest, a newspaper was able to list 200 successive "gangland slayings" over many years not one of which had been cleared.

No social policy for dealing with vocational crime offers certain solutions. Assigning more detectives to investigate professional predators, vigorous prosecution of those caught, and educating the public to be more wary may all reduce the appeal of crime as a vocation. We can reduce somewhat both professional and amateur predation if we make it more difficult to accomplish. Thus, burglar alarms are regularly improved, but sometimes their cost or inconvenience exceeds what is perceived as the cost of the burglary risk. In Europe it is often much more difficult to cash checks than in the United States and consequently forgery is less of a problem, but the citizens do not have as much convenience in procuring funds. In a sense, crime is an "overhead" cost item necessary for some of our freedom and efficiency. Thus whenever a store shifts from a salesclerk system to self-service, they suffer more losses from shoplifting, but this is more than offset by their savings in labor costs.

A certain amount of crime is to some extent the price we pay for an "open class" society, in which everyone is encouraged to aspire to the purchase of items he sees advertised in the mass media. Much publicity is given to wealthy celebrities of poor background. Since it is thus more difficult to accept low economic status, we should expect that there will always be some people tempted to take illegal short-cuts to high living standards, and that a few will be successful enough at it to become vocational predators.

Organized Illegal Sellers

Illegal sellers engaged in what is usually called *organized crime* are referred to here as *organized illegal sellers*. They are distinguished not only by illegal selling, but by conducting such activities as part of an organization of hierarchical complexity with a large number of participants, instead of alone or with a small number of partners. The organizations range in size from a few dozen to several hundred persons of diverse rank, each of whom has more or less specialized tasks. There is usually a rather extended chain of command, especially in the larger organizations, in which the lowest echelons rarely or never have contact with the top personnel. There may be national or even international federations of such organizations, but whether these are tightly knit and permanent in structure or loose-working partnerships is not known with certainty by anyone but the participants, and they are not telling.

Organized illegal selling in the United States is most extensively engaged in the provision of illegal gambling services, usurious loans, narcotics, and prostitution. It is believed that its peak size in terms of manpower occurred before the 1933 repeal of the Prohibition Amendment, which gave criminals a monopoly in the manufacture and distribution of alcoholic beverages. According to the President's Commission on Law Enforcement and the Administration of Justice (1967), gambling accounts for about seven-eighths of the income of organized crime in the United States, and the so-called "loansharking" or "juice" racket of loans at exorbitant rates has become second to gambling as a source of their income. It seems probable that if one possessed data on the many organizations involved in sale and distribution of illegal drugs, this would prove to be the second largest source of income from illegal sales in the 1970s.

Organized illegal selling has a large market because large segments of our population, if not a majority, utilize, or at least tolerate, goods and services which the law decries. It has been estimated that the gross annual income of these illegal business activities exceeds eight billion dollars, of which seven billion comes from gambling. Some estimates have been much higher than this; no one precisely knows the total. This is twice the value of estimated take in all crimes against property, including theft and pilfering by employees in business—which is seldom reported to the police (President's Commission, 1967).

Individual leaders of illegal selling organizations also operate legitimate businesses of all sorts with the help of their friends and relatives. They are especially prominent in wholesale liquor, pinball machine, and juke box distribution. They also own separate taverns and nightclubs, to which many originally moved as a logical transition from "speakeasy" operation under Prohibition. There is virtually no type of business in which they are not somewhere involved. They frequently head ostensibly member-owned unions and other enterprises, but instead of operating them primarily for membership benefit, they siphon off large personal incomes.

Whereas the leaders and most of the staff of criminal organizations were formerly resident in the slums, now they are dispersed throughout metropolitan areas, with the elite usually living in the suburbs and other prestigeful neighborhoods. The income from illegal businesses provides capital for investment in legitimate businesses, even banking and savings and loan organizations, as the leaders strive for a facade of respectability and try to keep their criminal activities secret.

Because the main activities of these individuals were originally illegal and usually still are, they tend to recruit staff accustomed to law violation and they engage in practices alien to conventional business. When operating outside the law, one cannot rely on the police and the courts to regulate competition, enforce contracts, and collect debts, so they maintain a private rule enforcement staff of vocational assaulters who inflict private social control measures, including corporal and capital punishment (Cressey, 1969). Because the organization recruits a staff willing to operate outside the law, an employment qualification with them is a record of predatory crime, as well as a demonstration of loyalty to other criminals by past acts in prison or by behavior under police interrogation. With such staff, illegal methods are used to expand both the illegal and the legal businesses of organized crime leaders, using threats, extortion, violence, and vandalism against competitors or reluctant customers. Many small restaurants and taverns, for example, get their towel services, garbage collection, and juke boxes from particular concerns—not because these firms have the most attractive prices and services, but because broken windows, fires, or worse can be expected if other firms are patronized.

The cohesiveness of a national organization in major criminal activities in the United States is uncertain. Our information comes from various informers, undercover law enforcement agents, and reporters. Probably none of these have a complete picture. The major recent source of information was the report of Joseph Valachi, a long-time, but minor, member of an organized criminal gang, who testified in 1963 before the McClellan Committee of the U.S. Senate. This has been mainly supplemented by summaries of tape recordings from electronic eavesdropping on organized crime leaders. From these diverse sources one infers that there is a national "commission" of organized crime "bosses," each of whom heads a regional unit known as a "family," which is centered in a metropolitan area. A few large areas, notably Greater New York, have several families. Some claim that the national unity of these criminal organizations is an illusion held by outsiders (Morris and Hawkins, 1970). They remain an important and distinct social problem whether their unity is national or merely regional.

The link of organized illegal selling with vocational assault becomes evident from waves of violence in particular regions, allegedly caused by internal wars that occur when an organization splinters into feuding factions, or one seeks the customers of the other. While some dismiss this as merely gangsters fighting one another, the values and skills it nurtures are also used against noncriminals. This is conspicuous in "racketeering"—extortion of "protection money" from businesses—and of "muscling in"—demanding partnership in someone else's business or in the leadership of a labor union local on threat of violence.

The leaders of organized crime almost always have ties with politics, and they have considerable skill in dealing with officials and various infl··-ential persons. They do favors for others in order to create goodwill, a. especially to make politicians "owe them" some favors. This is their b defense against prosecution. Indeed, it has been estimated that 15 percent of campaign contributions in local elections in the United States come from organized crime (Cressey, 1969, p. 243), but this is necessarily a wild guess. It is probably higher than this in some campaigns, and lower in others.

An illegal selling organization's distribution of money and favors for protection is only effective with carefully pursued strategies and tactics, to make expenditures profitable in the long run. Before a major investment is made in an illegal gambling center, for example, insurance against loss from law enforcement often requires that payoffs and understandings be negotiated in advance with policemen, other officials or politicians. Organized illegal sellers frequently contribute to both major political parties, and to several factions within particular parties, so that the organization is secure regardless of who wins elections. In criminal as in many legitimate businesses, goodwill is a major part of an organization's capital.

Although many senior members of criminal organizations shift to legitimate business enterprise and investments as their primary source of income and basic field of activity, a fundamental rule in organized crime is that once one is in, one cannot get completely out. A person may be encouraged to disengage himself from the organization when he is under police pressure, but this is probably considered a temporary and incomplete separation. The person who has been on the inside in the organization has lifetime obligations of both secrecy and availability for support and services when needed.

Since the 1963 confessions of Valachi, writers on organized crime have adopted his designation of any regional criminal organization as a "family." He described each family as directed by a "boss" with a few close associates, including legal and bookkeeping specialists; "buffers" to carry on communication between the boss and the line staff; "enforcers" to apply violence; "corrupters" to negotiate payoffs to officials and others. To a much greater extent now than formerly, individual members of these organizations and their business firms maintain legitimate records because the most successful prosecution against them from the 1930s to the 1950s was on income tax evasion.

There is an alleged link between American organized crime leaders and those in Sicily and southern Italy. Application of the term "Mafia" to the Italian-dominated criminal organizations in the United States is based on the long existence in Sicily of an organization of that name, which took over many businesses and terrorized and corrupted officials, but also provided social services to the poor. More recently the American organizations have been called "Cosa Nostra," which is Italian for "our group." The extent of Italian domination of organized crime in the United States is disputed, and it clearly varies greatly in different regions, and even in different cities or neighborhoods within some regions. Apparently in the 1920s, when Italians were predominantly poor immigrants in slum areas and had high crime rates, they "got in on the ground floor" in some illegal selling organizations and this reputation still persists now that people of Italian descent live in all communities, pursue all occupations, and have low crime rates. Italians arrived in the slums just as the Prohibition Amendment created a lucrative market for bootlegging. They are reported to have been successful in this organized activity partly because their patriarchal families emphasized obligations to kin (Finestone, 1967). Many from other ethnic groups, however, also have long engaged in organized illegal selling, and ethnic diversity increases as new selling groups develop in narcotics and other fields.

Social policy for reducing organized crime has reflected two highly contrasting philosophies. One approach emphasizes more rigorous law enforcement; the other stresses legalization of the illegal services to eliminate an exclusive market for criminal organizations.

Law enforcement against organized crime is extremely difficult because of the secrecy, the resources, and the tactics of these organizations. They have regularly used terror and assassination to prevent witnesses from testifying against them. Indeed, the targets of gangland murders are frequently persons who have been involved in organized crime who gang leaders fear will be tempted to cooperate with the police when under arrest in exchange for immunity from prosecution. Planned murder has even been achieved by criminal organizations while the victims were in penal custody, and it has frequently followed shortly upon their release. Law enforcement against gangland murderers is also discouraged by police and prosecutors, who share with most of the public an attitude of accepting assassinations of criminals by other criminals as "good riddance," and hope that they kill each other off.

To achieve increased success in prosecution of organized illegal sellers despite the dearth of complainants and witnesses willing to testify against them, prosecutors have requested and received resources and powers not usually employed against other types of criminals. These include authority to tap telephones and to install electronic eavesdropping equipment under secret court authorization. There have been persistent reports that investigators have used such procedures without court authorization in order to obtain leads to more adequate evidence, or a basis for requesting authorized eavesdropping and searches. As a result of such measures and of increased financial support for prosecution by the federal and many state and local government units, the rate of conviction for organized criminals has grown in recent years. Whether the actual volume of business conducted by organized crime has changed appreciably is uncertain. There is reason to believe that as long as the call for illegal goods and services exists, another criminal organization will expand to capture any market which law enforcement may prevent one organization from serving.

As indicated in discussing addiction-supported predation, our society tends to shift from permissiveness to prohibition to regulation. Reduction of organized criminal enterprises by legitimating the types of business they engaged in has occurred with the repeal of Prohibition, as well as with licensed or state-operated gambling in a few parts of the United States. Usually licensing regulations are designed to keep persons with a criminal record from operating businesses in these fields. When legalization of a product or service occurs, however, criminal organizations may have an advantage over competitors from the knowledge, experience, and resources they accumulated when providing the service illegally. They often evade licensing regulations by having persons without criminal records as the nominal heads of businesses. The Kefauver Committee revealed that this occurred following Prohibition, with criminal organizations operating many large breweries, liquor companies, and, especially, wholesale and retail distribution services for alcoholic beverages. Legalization, however, at least permits legitimate businessmen also to enter these fields. Even if there is not an immediate change of all services from a criminal to a noncriminal direction, their public operation fosters their gradual subjection to whatever formal and informal controls prevail in regular businesses (which, as mentioned when discussing confidence games, may still not eliminate some activities of questionable honesty).

To consider legalization one must examine the separate types of illegal service since each raises unique factual questions and value issues. Particularly relevant is the source of an estimated 85 percent of organized criminal income in the United States, the field of gambling. Actually, in the United States it is not gambling that is illegal so much as the time and place of gambling. In most states, one is permitted to bet on horseraces at the racetrack but not in off-track bookmaking establishments. One may play cards for money in a home with acquaintances and not risk prosecution, although in some jurisdictions this violates the law, but this is definitely illegal in a public place and likely to be prosecuted. Indeed, it is completely legal to gamble on the stock market, and a few states have government-operated lotteries and government-licensed centers for gambling. The most extensive and long-established legal gambling activity in the United States is in Nevada, but New Hampshire and New York established state-operated lotteries in the 1960s, and several other states are expected to follow this pattern in the 1970s. New York introduced legal off-track horse betting in 1970, and many jurisdictions either passively or statutorily permit raffles and other types of gambling by nonprofit organizations of diverse types.

The Kefauver Committee of the U.S. Senate estimated in the 1950s that there were 150,000 bookmakers in the United States and even a larger number employed in the "numbers racket," a poor man's lottery prevalent in slums. It was alleged that 10 to 20 percent of the income of these businesses was paid to the police for protection. The horseracing gambling services leased 16,000 miles of telephone and telegraph wires to transmit the outcomes of races to distant bookmakers in a matter of minutes. It was also alleged that a billion a year was spent on illegal, but tolerated, bingo— more than on professional baseball and boxing. No one really has enough information to make these estimates accurately; sample surveys of the public on the gambling activities in which they engage or of which they know would be suggestive. The existence of illegal horserace betting, however, is readily established in any city by the extent to which newspapers carry detailed racing news and tips even when no tracks are operating in their circulation area. In addition, it is clearly indicated at news stands by their daily sale of racing newspapers and tip sheets on tracks all over the country.

An interest in gambling appears to exist in almost all societies, from the present to the most ancient civilizations. Dice and other gambling devices are found in archeological diggings in Egypt, Babylonia, and China, and they were especially popular among the Greeks and the Romans. Gambling is generally viewed as pathological when pursued at great cost to self subsistence or support of one's family. Perhaps it is for this reason that it is more condoned in the leisure than in the laboring classes. The Puritan values of work and thrift are jeopardized by gambling and this appears to be the major motivation for making it relatively inconvenient to pursue for all but the leisured and affluent. Objections to legalization frequently describe pathological gamblers, who pursue gambling as an addiction, and seem neither to learn from losing nor to quit when winning. It should be noted that the above traits also characterize many persons in regular businesses; the line between the psychology of business success drives and gambling is often fuzzy, although businessmen are presumably more rational in choice of means.

In defense of licensed gambling one may argue that gambling serves a special function for those whose prospects for success are unpredictable or extremely low in legitimate economic competition. Talcott Parsons has asserted:

> ...it would be seriously disruptive to the society either to attempt to suppress gambling radically or to remove all the restrictions on it. On the one hand gambling performs important functions for large classes in the population, very similar to those of magic, as a kind of acting out of tensions which are symbolically at least associated with the economic sphere. On the other hand the values and sentiments which in one connection justify or rationalize the objections to gambling play a highly significant role in the general value system, and full permissiveness to gambling could not be allowed without undermining these values in other important spheres.
> ...It can probably be said that it is not merely a symptom of social

disorganization, but of a social structure which is sufficiently elastic, even at
the expense of serious cultural conflict, to relieve strains by permitting a good
deal of this type of behavior, and yet to keep it sufficiently within bounds
so that it is not too disruptive in the opposite direction. [Parsons, 1951,
pp. 307–308]

Systematic "market research" could provide a fuller understanding of
gambling and a more adequate basis for policy decisions. This could include
scientific sample surveys asking people to estimate the amount of time and
money spent by others in their neighborhood in various types of gambling
(assuming that they would not report so fully on themselves), then seeing
how this varies with neighborhoods and with population characteristics.
Ideally, such surveys should be conducted in areas which differ in the
availability of legalized gambling but are similar in other respects, or within
a jurisdiction before and after the legalization of gambling.

The forms of regulation may be extremely relevant. Sweden and
several other countries of Europe with extensive legal betting on the outcome
of athletic events and many countries with lotteries make the payoffs to
winners contingent on the amount bet on the different alternatives. This
payoff system, of course, characterizes betting at the horseraces in the
United States. The difference between European and American arrangements is that the American system involves a posting of the odds before the
event occurs, so that the gambler can infer how much he is likely to win
if he is successful on a given bet. It is claimed that when the odds are not
posted in advance so that the gambler can only guess at how many others
are betting on his choice—he does not know if he has a favorite or a long-
shot—he will bet more modestly than he would under the American system
(Allen, 1952).

Value-based arguments for legalization of gambling and other illegal
consumption sometimes claim a right of the individual to undertake whatever pleasure pursuits he desires, at whatever risks and costs he prefers, as
long as he does not hurt others. There is also the contention that making
these activities illegal provides a major income for organized crime, and
for its corruption of government. Availability of more facts on the dimensions of gambling and organized crime under various systems of limited
legalization would permit a more rational appraisal of the consequences
of different approaches to regulation from the standpoints of these value
concerns.

Usury, reputedly the second largest organized illegal sales activity in
the United States, is perhaps the most difficult to control. Its scope is limited,
nevertheless, by competition with banks and loan companies that have lower
interest rates. Usurers lend money to persons either unfamiliar with or too
poor to make good credit risks for legitimate lending agencies, or to persons
not wishing to reveal their financial problems to such agencies, perhaps

because their money needs stem from illegal activity. Credit counseling for the poor, and special aid programs for small businesses might permit some usurers' customers to borrow funds elsewhere.

Conservative economists since Malthus have argued against any restriction on interest rates because credit would probably be available from legitimate firms for many high-risk cases if interest were commensurate with the risk involved. One major stimulus to antiusury laws is misrepresentation of interest rates by loan companies and sellers of goods on credit, but this can be corrected through adequate and well-enforced "truth-in-lending" laws. The remaining competitive advantage of the illegal usurer, however, cannot be employed by legitimate business, and this may make any modification of antiusury laws irrelevant: the criminal can take greater credit risks because he is willing to use terror to assure collections. Much of the usury business is actually extortion of sums clearly beyond the commitments which the borrower understood he was making (Cressey, 1969, pp. 77–91). Only more vigorous law enforcement efforts can counteract organized criminal usury, and these efforts are handicapped by the usurers' intimidation of witnesses.

Legalization of opiate selling has already been discussed in the *addiction-supporting predation* section of this chapter, and legalization of marijuana and other "soft drugs" will be discussed in the last section, on *private criminal consumers*. All opiates could be freely administered by any physician to any medically registered addict in Britain until the 1960s, when the addiction rate doubled (though still clearly below that in the United States). Distribution of opiates by physicians was then restricted to designated clinics specializing in addiction treatment. These now endeavor to persuade addicts to change gradually from heroin or morphine injection to oral intake of methadone. The extensive provision of methadone as well as alternative treatments in the United States was recommended earlier in this chapter as a promising means of reducing addiction-supporting predation and prostitution.

Legalization of prostitution occurs in many large cities of Europe, once prevailed in several American communities, and still exists in Nevada on a county-option basis. One major argument for it has been its facilitation of regular medical examination to prevent the spread of venereal disease. Another argument is that efforts at suppressing prostitution, while repeated throughout history, have never succeeded. A third argument is that availability of prostitutes may reduce attempts at rape.

While law enforcement cannot eliminate prostitution, there is evidence that it can reduce the openness of solicitation by prostitutes (Walker, 1965, pp. 241–242). Sometimes only soliciting is made illegal rather than prostitution itself. One argument raised against legalizing prostitution, gambling, and narcotics use, which was also used against repeal of the Prohibition

Amendment, is that failure of the state to condemn these practices permits them to be more conspicuously available. Thus today one can find liquor sold in almost any commercial area, whereas before repeal of Prohibition its sale occurred in more hidden places. One can, of course, restrict the prominence of businesses without suppressing them, as most communities do in limiting the areas, hours, or advertising of liquor selling.

Ultimately arguments on reducing visibility of prostitution, even if one cannot suppress it entirely, depend on one's individual value position. Many believe that prostitution should not be legalized even if it cannot be adequately suppressed, because legalization is viewed as endorsing a demeaning of females. The main reason for diminished prostitution probably is not law enforcement efforts in any case, but competition due to freer attitudes towards sexual relations outside of marriage, and improvement and increased availability of contraception. These trends also foster much small group initiative in prostitution (Bryan, 1965), restricting by their competition the business prospects of large criminal organizations in this field.

The major threat to basic American values from organized illegal selling is probably the corruption of law enforcement and of government by bribes or terror. From corruption of officials, much other government service —such as efforts to combat predation, provide public housing, and aid the destitute—are impeded. Because legalization of their services would greatly reduce the resources of organized crime for corrupting government, many may endorse such legalization even when they abhor the services it provides, such as gambling or use of narcotics.

Avocational Predators

People who engage in property predation as a part-time activity to supplement their primary sources of income which are legitimate are referred to here as *avocational predators*. They correspond to what Morris (1965) called *avocational offenders*.

One of the most frequent criminal avocations is shoplifting, which a majority of Americans try as juveniles, and a smaller proportion—mainly housewives—continue as adults. Shoplifters are of all social class backgrounds. Adults usually operate alone. Generally they take items priced at less than ten dollars and victimize large stores so they do not readily perceive their offenses as injuring anyone, and do not think of themselves as criminal. This type of shoplifter is what Cameron (1964) called a "snitch," in the vernacular of store detectives, in contrast to the more vocationally oriented "boosters."

Most adult shoplifters (other than those who are addiction-supporting) seem to be stretching their purchasing power somewhat, rather than procuring necessities. Indeed, many carry more than enough funds to pay for the items they steal, but seem enthralled by their success at "getting away with it," and pursue theft as a sort of game. This psychological preoccupation is popularly known as *kleptomania,* but has been little studied as mental disease, perhaps because avocational shoplifting usually terminates once the offender is caught. Although theft by persons not destitute is viewed by others as evidence of deepseated irrationality, it apparently only involves persistence of a behavior pattern while it is successful, with no strong dependence on it. A majority are not prosecuted, but apprehension and the threat of exposure are sufficient to reform them. This illustrates a principle noted by Chambliss (1967) : Deterrence works where an offense is instrumental (a means to an end, rather than an end in itself) and where there is low commitment to the offense (e.g., it is not used for necessities).

Another frequent criminal avocation is pilfering by employees. Some investigators claim that this is a greater source of loss, even in department stores, than shoplifting. Again corporations are the preferred victims. It illustrates the principle of the American value system demonstrated by Smigel (1956) : Abhorrence of stealing varies inversely with the size of the victim organization. That is why avocational theft from large corporations or from the government is compatible with a conception of self as non-criminal. Theft and other crimes are apparently not conceived abstractly by the public. They are seen as personal relationships between offenders and victims, with moral outrage arising from empathy with the victim. For impersonal organizations there is little empathy. (For further discussion, see Smigel and Ross, 1970.)

Most so-called "white collar crime" is also avocational, rather than a primary source of income. This type of offense was defined in the classic work by Edwin H. Sutherland (1949, p. 9) as ". . .a crime committed by a person of respectability and high social status in the course of his occupation." He illustrated it by data on restraint of trade through monopoly and collusion to drive out competition, infringement of patent rights, misrepresentation in advertising, unfair labor practices, and financial manipulations. All of these violate laws providing specific penalties, but the laws are usually unenforced, or their penalties are too mild for deterrence. The fines, levied against corporations rather than individuals, are not sufficient as an expense to make the illegal practices unprofitable. Because these crimes are pursued routinely, as traditional practice in some businesses, because in any particular business the separate victims are affected by a higher cost on only one component of their living expenses, and because specific individual victims do not have the resources to prosecute, these crimes are generally ignored in portrayals of the national crime problem. Their total economic impact, however, may be greater than that of all other types of crime combined, including gambling and other organized illegal selling.

The heavy electrical equipment antitrust cases of 1961 (Geis, in Clinard and Quinney, 1967) were among the first instances in which executives of major corporations were imprisoned for illegal activities of the firms that employed them. An increase in "class suits" against corporations on behalf of many victims may also reduce the immunity of "white collar" offenders from effective sanctions. Whether these measures will increase sufficiently to warrant drastic overhaul of Sutherland's conclusions on public indifference to "white collar" crime remains to be seen. It appears that prevention of such offenses requires both a change in prevalent values regarding them, and augmentation of state resources for policing and prosecuting them. If these measures develop, such crimes will probably diminish markedly because they will become unprofitable and because the stigma of criminality would impede the legitimate business activities of the corporations now committing these crimes without penalty.

Crisis-Vacillation Predators

Persons long committed to conformity to the law, who shift to predation in an effort to resolve an unusual crisis in their lives are referred to here as *crisis-vacillation predators*. This type corresponds to what Morris (1965) and others have called *situational offenders* and Gibbons (1968) called *"one-time loser" property offenders*. Its clearest exemplification is the embezzler, a person in a position of trust who fraudulently appropriates for himself the money or property entrusted to him.

In order to be in a position to commit major embezzlement, a person must have had a lifetime of apparent trustworthiness. This is the only way in which embezzlers can have obtained their typical positions, for example, as officials of banks or savings and loan associations, treasurers or comptrollers of government or educational agencies, lawyers administering trust funds, or salesmen of jewelry or other highly valuable articles. They are usually good "mixers," popular in elite social circles, and often considered the junior executives "most likely to succeed." Cressey (1953) found that all persons who shifted from trustworthiness to embezzlement clearly went through three stages somewhat distinct in their memories, prior to actually violating their trust. These were:

A. Incurring What They Perceive as an Unsharable Problem. Generally this is something which, the offenders believed, would severaly jeopardize their careers unless kept secret. For example, a business or political executive incurs excessive debts in putting up a front of affluence and generosity in hopes of achieving "connections" for higher income opportunity, or a banking or brokerage employee who has made a poor investment has large gambling losses, or is threatened with exposure of a sexual or other indiscretion which he fears would ruin his career if exposed. Usually he stalls exposure by making payment promises he cannot keep or by partial payments which only deepen his financial dilemma.

B. Conceiving of Embezzlement as a Solution to the Problem. At some point in mulling over his crisis the prospective embezzler realizes the possibility of committing his crime. Sometimes this stage is not very distinct because the crime requires very little imagination, but sometimes it involves elaborate bookkeeping entries to cover up removal of funds or property.

C. Developing a Rationalization for the Offenses. For a person with a high commitment to conformity to undertake a crime he must be able to conceive of it as compatible with his image of himself as a law-respecting person. Sometimes much time elapses between his conception of the embezzlement and his acceptance of it as morally justifiable behavior in his case. Rationalizations typically represent the offense as borrowing which will be secretly repaid so no one will know the difference, and as money "coming to him" because he has not been compensated adequately for his services.

Another group of crisis vacillators are the persons without criminal backgrounds who commit rash crimes when they conceive of their economic condition as desperate. These commit a growing proportion of armed robberies of banks and other financial institutions. The impersonal corporation with large sums of cash on hand appeals as a target for predation because it is assumed that no individuals will be severely injured by the organization's losses, and because enough money is expected from the robbery to solve all the offender's woes at once. Use of unloaded or toy guns is most frequent when robbers are non-vocational.

Although wider acceptance of confidential counseling on personal problems might conceivably reduce the frequency of financial desperation, the basic cause of avocational and crisis-vacillation property crimes appears generally to be undue emphasis on economic success and conspicuous consumption in our culture. Punishment merely by arrest and exposure seems adequate for terminating criminality by crisis-vacillation offenders, for they have extremely high success rates on probation and parole. Usually many people to whom they previously would not dare reveal their difficulties rally to aid them when their problems are exposed following arrest and prosecution. Many embezzlers are even rehabilitated by paternalistic employers who discover the offense and do not report it, but work out a long-term restitution plan for their employee.

Quasi-Insane Assaulters

A residual and diverse group of offenders falls into the group referred to here as *quasi-insane assaulters.* It is appreciably less numerous than any other type we have distinguished, but attracts more public attention than all other types combined. These are the murderers and sexual assaulters who do not clearly fit the subculture of violence pattern, for they are not "understandable" in common-sense terms as being provoked to their offenses by an exaggeration of ordinary anger or lust. Perhaps because they seem to have no justification for their crimes they outrage public sensibilities most. Each such case is reported for weeks on the front pages of newspapers, on television, and often in magazines during the course of efforts to apprehend and convict the assaulters, and again, when they are considered for parole or for commutation of a death sentence.

The law provides that a person can only be considered criminal if he is judged to have been sane at the time he committed his offense. In Britain about a third and in the United States about 5 percent of those charged with murder are found not guilty on grounds of insanity. Sanity, however, is diversely defined, and in most application to crime has great ambiguity (for a fuller discussion see Mechanic, 1970, pp. 138–143). It is a legal rather than a psychiatric concept, but the courts call upon psychiatrists for advice before deciding that anyone is insane, although psychiatrists disagree radically with each other as to the sanity of many criminals. Therefore, it is reasonable to view many who have been held by the courts to be legally responsible as actually of debatable sanity, or at least as quasi-insane.

The most highly publicized murder cases are almost all of this type— for example, England's "Jack the Ripper"; the Loeb and Leopold, Heirens, and William Speck cases in Illinois; Boston's "Strangler"; the Chessman and Manson "family" cases in California. Although in some of these doubt is maintained as to the guilt of those convicted, there is little doubt that whoever committed the offenses of which they were accused was not of ordinary criminal mentality. While not a daily event anywhere, on many days of each month newspapers reveal other cases of this type, usually publicized nationally or even internationally. As Kenefick's summary of the literature indicates (Glaser, Kenefick and O'Leary, 1966, Part VI), violent crimes that are not "an appropriate reaction, under the given circumstances, to a specific situation," have received extremely diverse and speculative explanations by psychiatrists. Factors emphasized include brain damage, severe depression, and paranoid schizophrenia.

The offenders we are discussing here are typically detached and deluded about the criminal acts they commit. They conceive of their crimes in fantasy and abstraction as people do in the daydreams or nightmares of normal life, but they lose the capacity to separate dream from reality. Sometimes they view the crime as outside themselves, as though watching a movie, but they often develop paranoid-like delusions of their cunning or courage in conceiving of these offenses and, subsequently, in not being caught or convicted. Delusions of persecution—not necessarily by their victims, but by others who did not properly recognize their abilities and reward them—also provide rationalizations for the offenses.

Frequently quasi-insane group offenders report individually having had misgivings about going through with the crime, but not being willing to "lose face" before the others by suggesting that they abandon their plan, and not really being aware of what they had done until afterwards. Once criminal acts are initiated, panic often causes the offender to kill all victims or observers in order to remove witnesses who might identify him. From a literary point of view Truman Capote's *In Cold Blood* (1965) is perhaps the best of many efforts to describe the mentality of this type of criminal.

Typical of the quasi-insane rapist is a gross misconception of female psychology. Several such multivictim assaulters whom I interviewed for the Illinois Parole and Pardon Board were reared with no sex instruction or experience, received only distorted ideas on sex from other boys, and assumed that females are aroused sexually in the same manner as inexperienced males. They actually expected the female strangers whom they suddenly grabbed from behind to become sexually cooperative, and were angered when this did not occur. Their sense of being humiliated as males as a result of being unable to force a woman into intercourse (an impossible task in most cases if the female is conscious and extreme pain is not inflicted), led to their becoming increasingly violent and using weapons in subsequent attacks on women. Possibly sex education and even legalized prostitution might reduce these offenses. (One such offender told me that he was enlightened on the availability of sex without assault while out on bail pending trial for rape when his father took him to a house of prostitution.)

A distinctly abnormal behavior syndrome represented in all state prisons is the aged molester of children. These are typically men in their fifty's, sixty's or seventy's—though occasionally younger—who sexually fondle very young girls, often of preschool age. They have one of the highest rates of repetition of the same offense after release from incarceration of any category of prisoner. Most claim to have been only harmlessly fondling the child and deny any indecent action or intent. While some may indeed be victims of hysterical accusation, when the offense is charged repeatedly against the same person in separate locations and with different children it seems unlikely that they were convicted when innocent of abnormal sexual activity. Frequently, however, they will be allowed to plead guilty to a lesser charge, such as disorderly conduct or loitering in a schoolyard, as a means of expediting trial or because of doubts as to the seriousness of their offenses (Sudnow, 1965).

Hysterical reactions by family or others often cause greater injury to the child than the actions of the criminal. The psychological injury is minimized if the child can be led to view the offender's acts as improper but not terrifying. Nevertheless, there are some molesters who do serious physical damage and even inflict death, though these are a small minority. Prevention focuses on teaching children not to accept gifts or rides from strangers. New Jersey and several other states have developed extensive psychiatric treatment services for this type of criminal, and report achieving a marked reduction in recidivism rates. With the older offenders the offense is ascribed to anxiety over decline in their sexual potency with age, and a compensating effort to obtain sexual stimulation from a female love object more accessible and less demanding than an adult woman. Therapy focuses on getting them to accept potency changes due to age as normal, and to assess their sexual adequacy by more realistic standards.

In considering social policy on quasi-insane offenders it is important not to generalize about all crime from such sensational but relatively rare criminals. It is common for most people in a metropolitan region of several million population to take major precautions against assault and to advocate drastic revisions of police and penal practices following publicity about the acts of one or two quasi-insane offenders, as when the "Boston Strangler" was rampant. Yet risks of victimization are hundreds or thousands of times as great from offenders of quite different types against whose offenses other policy would be more appropriate. The vicious assault by a stranger is seized upon by demagogues, but the occurrence of such crimes is a small fraction of the total crimes against persons, and no policy will readily diminish them from their present low frequency in most areas at most times.

The diversity of those who commit quasi-insane assaults, as well as their rarity, make it difficult to generalize a policy for them. Many members of quasi-insane offense groups who appear to have been dependent person-alities attached to more schizophrenic leaders seem to be shocked into a realistic view of their offenses—as soon as they have committed them in some cases, and after apprehension and confinement in others—particularly if they are separated from their criminal associates. These offenders—as well as rapists with no other criminal record—have very high success rates on parole, even those who had committed numerous and vicious rape attempts before their first arrest. Of course, their advanced age at release, due to their long confinement, may be a factor in their success rate.

If offenders manifest clear symptoms of brain damage, schizophrenia, or other mental ailments during confinement they are transferred to the psychiatric hospital which is part of most prison systems, and confined in the security unit or other component of a state mental hospital after they complete their prison terms. Social policies for prevention of such offenses or for treatment of the offenders are those which are appropriate for these mental illnesses generally, and are the concern of a separate book in this series (Mechanic, 1970).

Addicted Performers

Of the total arrests reported by police agencies to the U.S. Department of Justice for tabulation in *Uniform Crime Reports* in 1969, 24 percent were for drunkenness, 10 percent for disorderly conduct, 6 percent for driving under the influence of alcohol, and 2 percent for vagrancy. Presumably most of the drunkenness and driving arrests and many of those for disorderly conduct and vagrancy were for the behavioral manifestations of an addiction to alcohol. Most of these arrest percentages were lower than in preceding years. In 1960, 36 percent of reported arrests were for vagrancy. Apart from percentages of the total, the actual number of arrests for drunkenness and vagrancy has declined in recent years, despite increases in total arrests of all types and growth in the United States population.

This decline in arrests for illegal performances due largely to alcoholism probably represents neither a change in the prevalence of this addiction, nor an alteration in the behavior of people when drunk, but instead a change in police conduct. Such change was especially encouraged by two federal appelate court decisions in 1966, which declared that public drunkenness caused by the disease of alcoholism is involuntary, hence not grounds for arrest. These partially reversed a long-standing common law principle that all drunkenness is voluntary, thus not an excuse for any crime (Hutt, 1967). Their impact has been great despite *Powell* v. *Texas* in 1968, in which the Supreme Court rejected mandatory civil confinement of alcoholics for treatment in lieu of prosecution under the criminal law.

The traditional and still widespread government reaction to people behaving publicly in a drunken manner consists of rounding them up in the streets and parks where they are most concentrated, and jailing them overnight or for a few days. This is done primarily in the so-called "skid row" areas of our large cities—generally located just outside the central business district—where chronic alcoholics live on the streets and in cheap "flophouses" and missions established there to serve them. Arresting for drunkenness is aptly called a "revolving door" procedure, for jailing seems to have no impact on alcoholism; releasees from jail usually return immediately to their previous way of life.

Programs for the treatment of alcoholism, notably Alcoholics Anonymous, were discussed earlier in our section on addiction-supporting predators. Policies for coping with drunken behavior in public involve quite different issues. What has been increasingly suggested, on both legal and practical grounds, is: (a) more tolerance for drunken comportment when it clearly does not harm anyone; (b) provision of services for relief and rehabilitation of drunken persons, on a purely voluntary basis, rather than burdening the police, courts, jails, and the alcoholics themselves with the futile consequences of classifying public drunkenness as a crime. Morris and Hawkins engagingly propose:

> For the police lockups, courts, and jails we would substitute community-owned overnight houses capable of bedding down insensible or exhausted drunks. For the police and the paddy wagons we would substitute minibuses, each with a woman driver and two men knowledgeable of the local community in which the minibus will move. A woman is preferred to a man... because it is our experience that the presence of a woman has an ameliorative effect on the behavior of males, even drunken males.
> The minibus would tour the skid row area.... If there be a protest

or resistance by a drunk, cowardice and withdrawal would control our team's actions; if there be assaults...a police transceiver will call those who will attend to it; if there be unconsciousness or drunken consent, the minibus will deliver the body to the overnight house.

If there be talk by the drunk the next day of treatment...let him... be taken to whatever social assistance and alcohol treatment facilities are available. Indeed, let such assistance be offered if he fails to mention them; but let them never be coercively pressed. [Morris and Hawkins, 1970, pp. 7–8]

The police have long provided this service, in essence, for the more affluent drunks in better residential areas; instead of locking them up, they take them home. In 1966, under a federal grant, a thirty-bed Detoxification and Diagnostic Evaluation Center was established for alcoholics in a St. Louis hospital to which police from skid row precincts bring drunks instead of arresting them. The police complete an admission form at the center and phone headquarters to see if the drunks are wanted for any offense, but eliminating the normal booking procedure reduces police time per case 50 percent, and also relieves courts and jails. The drunks are offered seven days of service, and over 90 percent stay for this period. Their physical health improves markedly, and many are successfully referred to employment, housing, and various continuing alcoholism treatment organizations. While 46 percent of the center's 1967 dischargees had been arrested in the three months prior to their admission, only 13 percent were arrested in the same period afterwards. In a four-month follow-up of 200 male releasees, of whom only 160 were actually located, it was estimated that 50 percent demonstrated significant overall improvement from the standpoints of reduced drinking, better health, more employment, and other variables (Law Enforcement Assistance Administration, 1970).

Somewhat analogous procedures were initiated in New York under the Vera Foundation's Bowery Project, and federal funds to cities for the establishment of such centers became available with the Alcoholic Rehabilitation Act of 1968. Arrests for illegal performance still occur, but those reflecting only distaste for the impoverished alcoholic are diminishing, and the public's interest is best served when arrests are replaced by transportation to centers like that pioneered by St. Louis.

Private Illegal Consumers

Persons who persist in private illegal consumption—not predation-supported—are referred to here as *private illegal consumers*. They include most adult users of marijuana, LSD, amphetamines, and other relatively non-addictive drugs, as well as the frequently addictive use of barbiturates. Also appropriately included are those who willingly engage in private homosexual acts, and those who purchase illegal gambling or prostitution services.

Although some of these activities, such as marijuana use, result in many arrests, surveys of the general population suggest that the number of adults arrested for any of these types of consumption is less than 1 percent of those who engage in them. For some of these crimes, such as possession of marijuana, the prescribed penalties are extremely severe, while for the others, penalties are much milder. It would be difficult to demonstrate that the social or personal damage resulting from marijuana use is greater than that from the other drugs listed above, or even than alcohol which breaks down behavior controls more quickly and drastically (Weil, *et al*, 1968; Crancer, *et al*, 1969).

Public opinion polls late in 1969 indicated that one-eighth of Americans in their twenties had used marijuana, and the proportions were greater among 18- and 19-year-olds, as well as among all ages in college. The percent of college students who admitted to the Gallup poll that they had tried marijuana increased from 5 in 1967 to 22 in 1969 to 42 in 1970. This means that in future years an extremely large percentage of the influential voters will have had first-hand experience with a type of felonious behavior that virtually never does any harm which is apparent to them. Consequently, enforcing current laws against marijuana use will become increasingly difficult, and will alienate more of the population from law-making and enforcing agencies. Regardless of one's judgment of marijuana use, it is apparent that it will become increasingly controversial, and that the controversy will probably be resolved—as was that over alcohol use—by shifting from a policy of prohibition to one of regulation. The latter will probably control the strength and method of distribution of marijuana by licensed dealers.

Illegal use of amphetamines and barbiturates involves complicity of the leading American drug manufacturers, who market several times as much of these drugs as are prescribed by physicians—as they well know. Through illegal diversion at the wholesale or retail pharmacist level, and through sale to Mexican dealers who sell to Americans in wholesale lots at the bordertowns, large quantities are illegally distributed in the United States. Some varieties of substance abuse, such as glue-sniffing, appear to occur almost exclusively in the juvenile years. Other types, notably use of methedrine ("speed"), apparently diminish rapidly with age in early adulthood, but by no means disappear. Addiction to barbiturates such as sleeping pills is common at many age levels, and is often alternated daily with use of amphetamines ("pep-pills") to stay awake.

In New York, San Francisco, and Los Angeles conspicuously, and in all large cities to some extent, "gay bars" and other places exist in which homosexuals openly display their sexual preferences. There are also public communications of their interests, such as advertising and parades despite laws proscribing homosexual acts. Illinois in 1961 adopted a criminal code to replace all prior descriptions of crimes in separate statutes, and this code's specifications for *deviate sexual conduct* offenses all included either an age discrepancy in which one party was under 18, use of force or threat of force, or performance in a public place. By omission, therefore, the homosexual acts of consenting adults in private became legal. There is no reason to believe that the rate of homosexuality thereafter increased in Illinois any more than in other states where this type of behavior remained criminal.

Because drug offenses involve very compact substances that are taken voluntarily and privately, the police learn of them only by spying or entrapment. These methods are also necessary in most police action against homosexuality. This contrasts with predatory offenses or illegal performances, where a victim or complainant calls the police, or the police observe the crime in a public place. To catch drug users or homosexuals, police must usually have a detective befriend them and feign an interest in participating in their illegal activities, or induce some of them to be witnesses against the others. This leads to frequent reports of abuses, such as informers of doubtful credibility, bribery of police or of informers, and extortion of funds from offenders on threat of arrest or of informing. The policing difficulties also mean that only a small proportion of the actual offenders can be arrested and successfully prosecuted even with a large and costly police effort.

An alternative to defining these private illegal consumptions as criminal is to view them, like alcoholism, as problems in public health. From an ethical standpoint, it is argued that if a person wishes to abuse his body by taking drugs, by overeating, by smoking heavily, or in any other manner that does not hurt others, this is his right. The currently illegal consumptions can be opposed by the state through education against them, and by closer regulation of the distribution of drugs. To charge the police and courts with prosecuting these consumptions as crimes, however, is to enforce the law very haphazardly and to encourage abuses in law enforcement. These problems promote disrespect for the law, and add to the work overload of police and courts.

THE POLICE

A criminal's first contact with the state is usually with the police. While crime is any act for which the state may impose a penalty, penalties are only possible for those acts which result in police action. Hence police define crime operationally. Of course, courts order and corrections carry out ultimate state penalties, but, with minor exceptions, they cannot deal with anyone until he is brought to them by the police. Many whom the police detain, however, will never even get to a court. To understand the behavior of the police, their problems, and their crucial importance as gatekeepers of the criminal justice system, it is necessary to be aware of the history of our method of policing.

The Atomization of American Police Power

The United States has almost half a million police officers but they are distributed in about forty thousand autonomous police agencies, most of them a part of municipal government. No other country in the world has this separation of police forces. Our system has a relatively brief history—it is only about one hundred and fifty years old. It began in Britain, but in many ways it has changed there more than it has here.

Prior to the nineteenth century, policing in Britain and in its colonies was done primarily by officers of the courts. Some of them, like the sheriffs, obtained their positions by descent, while others, such as constables, bailiffs, and coroners, were appointed by those of the gentry who held judicial and sheriff offices. They were supplemented by the royal military forces when necessary, but a distinctive feature of the evolution of democracy in Britain, beginning in 1215 with its specification in Magna Carta, was local control of lower level judicial agencies and their associated police. By contrast, police of other countries, both monarchies and republics, were part of the military, or were nationally organized offshoots from it.

In Britain, citizens were long involved in local law enforcement. Under the Common Law principle of *posse comitatus,* officers of the law could conscript any citizen into immediate criminal-chasing service. Anyone who saw a thief was to give "hue and cry"—to yell "STOP THIEF!"—and other citizens were obliged to help catch the accused. With the growth of commerce in large cities there were more and more problems with theft from shops and market places, and voluntary "watch and ward" organizations developed. Later, merchants in certain areas collectively hired watchmen, or professional watchmen organizations contracted with shopkeepers. One of the most famous early watchmen's organizations, the Bow Street Runners, was founded by the author and magistrate, Henry Fielding. Persistent crime problems, however, led merchants to pressure the government to take over policing, and in 1829 Prime Minister Robert Peel succeeded in having the London Municipal Police established. They are still known as "Bobbies" after him. Peel's effort met much opposition because of the bad reputation of military police forces on the Continent, and the Bobbies were at first not allowed to wear uniforms.

American municipalities soon followed the London model with New York establishing its city police in 1844, and Chicago in 1851. Federal policing in the territories which were not yet states had begun earlier, using officers of the territorial circuit courts known as U.S. marshals, augmented by military units. The Texas Rangers were founded in 1835. State police, introduced in the early twentieth century to assist in strikebreaking, later became primarily occupied with highway patrol. We now have several specialized national police forces, such as the Federal Bureau of Investigation, the Secret Service, and the Postal Inspection, Customs and Immigration Services.

For fear of the power of a police state, there has long been vehement opposition to any suggestion that police in the United States be integrated into single national or state forces. Gordon Misner, a leading American authority on the police, has stated:

> Our traditional pattern of law enforcement is a historical accident, followed by no other civilized nation in the world. Regardless of size, location in relation to other units of general local government, or financial resources, each unit of local government is deemed "capable" of administering basic law enforcement within the confines of its own jurisdiction. [1960, p. 497]

The Multiplicity of Police Concerns

Personnel directing any organization usually have multiple concerns, and a police force is no exception. First, *selection* of the matters to which they will give various amounts of attention is necessary, because any community seeks to control more unlawful conduct than can be completely controlled by whatever police resources it chooses to provide. The police, for example, cannot keep all staff always working on any unsolved crime, and sometimes they cannot give the fullest service on all calls they receive at once. Second, and related to the foregoing, they have the problem of *efficiency,* of achieving maximum effectiveness with the resources available to them. Third, they are expected to conform with laws and customs of *fairness* in procedure, which may not always coincide with what they perceive as maximum efficiency. Fourth, they have problems of *system maintenance,* which means that they need public support, but more immediately, support of executives who can fire police chiefs, and of legislative bodies who pass on police budgets. They must also have good staff morale. To understand why the criminal justice system operates as it does at the police, and also at the court and correction levels, one must analyze how the decisions of their personnel are affected by the four types of concern outlined here.[1]

The notion that the criminal justice system selects its clients seems alien to our ideal of a government of laws, not men. The professional image promoted by many police forces and police professional organizations is that of nondecision-makers who merely enforce the legislature's decisions that are enacted as law. As Herman Goldstein has noted (1963), the police refuse to acknowledge existence of a policy other than that of full enforcement of the law because (to paraphrase):

1. To admit any nonenforcement is to suggest that the police are not doing their job, even if full enforcement is impossible.
2. To discuss discretion suggests that the police are not impartial.
3. To spell out criteria for discretion seems presumptuous in an administrative body, since they could then be accused of usurping legislative powers.
4. They cannot readily specify the actual operation and limits of discretion in writing, due to the vagueness of some laws and the necessary subjectivity of most judgment in using discretion.
5. An officer's oath is to enforce all the laws, so he cannot be forced to exercise discretion; in fact, it may be illegal to ask him to use discretion.
6. To endorse discretion may foster corruption that is excused as discretion.
7. There is a fear that articulate interest groups who want certain laws enforced will react vigorously if told specifically that the police are not interested in enforcing them.

[1] For the analysis in this paragraph, elaborated in the rest of this chapter, and in the next two chapters, I am indebted to communication in the early 1960s with Professor Frank J. Remington of the University of Wisconsin Law School. Which parts of this formulation are his contributions and which are mine, I do not now know.

An extensive survey of actual police decisions, conducted by the American Bar Foundation under the field direction of Frank Remington, with arrest decisions analyzed by Wayne R. LaFave (1965), made it apparent that some police discretion is inevitable because (to paraphrase) :

1. Most laws have ambiguous borderlines, so police must decide when they are applicable (e.g., disorderly conduct).
2. Police resources are limited.
3. The police receive social pressure to take into account special mitigating or aggravating factors, such as whether an accused is a "good citizen," or a juvenile, or a person of bad reputation.
4. Frequently the victim changes his mind about pressing charges and cooperating in prosecution, after police investigation has begun.
5. In view of the above, human reactions of the police to respect or disrespect from others, their personal likes and antipathies, and any class or other group prejudices they may hold inevitably affect their exercise of discretion to some extent.

James Q. Wilson (1968) has noted that the police are one of the few organizations where discretion increases as one goes down the staff hierarchy. Perhaps this is because it is the action of the lowest-ranked police that is least often visible in the mass media or to higher officials. In most matters, higher officials know only of those police actions that the lower officers report.

One reason for concern with efficiency is that any police decision to prosecute a law violator is a decision to commit many hours to the task. For major felony cases in which a trial results, collection and presentation of evidence may require hundreds of man-days. Large police forces have specialized units such as homicide squads and robbery details for serious crimes so that patrolmen are not removed from their beats for evidence collection in such offenses, even if they were initially involved in the investigation.

Actually, most calls for police services are not for criminal matters. A sample of 801 phone calls to Syracuse police revealed that about 40 percent were for law enforcement, but many of these were inquiries on traffic tickets, and about 60 percent were for various personal problems, such as getting an ambulance, tracing missing children, alleviating fears, mediating family quarrels, and removing drunks. Most calls were from seven to ten P.M., and even later on weekends, but they continued all night (Cumming, *et al,* 1965). The police are the only agency available twenty-four hours a day seven days a week for a vast variety of emergencies. Police services are less necessary when people have close relationships with their neighbors or have relatives nearby, but these conditions are diminishing in our impersonal metropolises. Commentators have referred to these functions which have nothing to do with law enforcement as *peacekeeping* or *order maintenance,* but no label adequately connotes all of them. They include directing, assisting, warning, escorting, transporting, mediating, consoling, and counseling.

In areas where gambling and prostitution are prevalent, and the penalty on conviction is only a minor fine, police often deem it most efficient to harass the offenders whenever these crimes become so visible as to elicit complaints, rather than to seek convictions. Harassment, of course, is not regulated by the courts, so it can readily become a means of shakedowns and a source of corruption.

Problems of fairness and legality also arise because the many services other than law enforcement which the public demands of the police are not regulated by any law. In many of these services police can use their potential to arrest as a threat to achieve cooperation, or cooperation is given them automatically because their possession of this power is known. Thus, peacekeeping by ordering potential troublemakers to leave a location is not legal, and may be converted quickly by the police to questionable law enforcement if noncooperation occurs. Conversely, conflicts among citizens over law violations are often mediated by the police as though they were only matters of peacekeeping. Furthermore, much taking of persons into custody by the police, as in public drunkenness arrests, is more concerned with service than with law enforcement. If there is an address to which the drunk can be transported, or if there is a relative who can be called, this is frequently the preferred solution. Sometimes the drunk is taken to jail as a welfare matter to prevent his freezing to death, or being robbed or run over (Bittner, 1967).

The basic norms for law enforcement are provided by several of the first ten amendments to the U.S. Constitution which comprise the Bill of Rights. The Fourth Amendment reads:

> The right of the people to be secure in their persons, houses, papers, and effects, against unreasonable searches and seizures, shall not be violated, and no warrants shall issue but upon probable cause, supported by oath or affirmation, and particularly describing the place to be searched and the persons or things to be seized.

The Fifth Amendment adds, among other things, the statement that:

> No person...shall be compelled in any criminal case to be a witness against himself, nor be deprived of life, liberty, or property, without due process of law.

The Sixth Amendment provides that:

> ...the accused shall enjoy the right to a speedy and public trial by an impartial jury of the State and district wherein the crime shall have been committed,... and to be informed of the nature and cause of the accusation; to be confronted with the witnesses against him; to have compulsory process for obtaining witnesses in his favor, and to have the assistance of counsel for his defense.

Also of importance is Section One of the Fourteenth Amendment, which reads:

> All persons born or naturalized in the United States, and subject to the jurisdiction thereof, are citizens of the United States and of the State wherein they reside. No State shall make or enforce any law which shall abridge the privileges or immunities of citizens of the United States; nor shall any State deprive any person of life, liberty, or property, without due process of law; nor deny to any person within its jurisdiction the equal protection of the laws.

While the Constitution is the basic law of the land, and much of the Bill of Rights is incorporated in many state constitutions, there has been considerable disagreement as to how some of the above provisions should be interpreted. An *exclusionary rule* against use in the courts of evidence obtained or arrests made illegally was adopted in federal courts in 1914, and subsequently in about half the states. In its 1961 *Mapp* v. *Ohio* decision, however, the Supreme Court interpreted the due process clause of the Fourteenth Amendment as extending the exclusion of illegally obtained evidence to all the states. In the 1963 *Gideon* v. *Wainwright* case, they insisted that every accused has the right to counsel at trial. In 1964, *Escobedo* v. *Illinois* established that a person has a right to a lawyer even prior to trial, when being questioned in police custody. Finally, in 1966 *Miranda* v. *Arizona* decreed that the accused must be advised by the police of his right to counsel and his right to be silent, before they interrogate him.

It has been clearly established that the provisions of the Bill of Rights cited above, strictly interpreted, were widely ignored, even in states having the exclusionary rule (LaFave, 1965). They are still followed in only a minority of police-citizen encounters, despite the controversial Supreme Court rulings of the 1960s (Black and Reiss, 1967). The warrant, specified in the Fourth Amendment, is a device to involve the judge in the officer's decision to arrest, and originated when policing was primarily by officers of the court in predominantly rural or small communities of past eras which lacked the rapid vehicles and high rates of geographic mobility which characterize today's population. Warrants are still used when arrest, search, or seizure actions are highly deliberate parts of a plan to prosecute, especially against someone with strong defense counsel; but they are not used routinely because of their conflict with police interest in efficiency.

As the procedure required to obtain a conviction becomes more time-consuming and less certain in outcome, the percentage of contacts with citizens in which the police are concerned with obtaining a conviction necessarily diminishes. When police do not seek a conviction they are not regulated closely by the norms of proper procedure since they will not lose a case for improper procedure if they do not take it to court, and they can only be sanctioned for illegal acts if the accused seeks to sue them, which is usually difficult and unlikely. Thus, court efforts to make police more lawful may have the effect of making them more lawless.

Courts have ruled that the police have a right to arrest someone whenever they have "probable cause" to believe he has committed a serious crime, and that whenever this occurs, they have a right to search his person and immediate surroundings. Jerome H. Skolnick (1966, pp. 212–218) observed, after extensive travels with police patrols, that if they find evidence of crime after proceeding to detain and to search without probable cause, they can usually invent cause afterwards. The policeman's "working personality," he asserts, is characterized by suspicion, fear, and social isolation from persons not in the police force. The officer is always anxious to use whatever method he deems appropriate to reduce what he perceives as a danger to himself. He differentiates people as being suspicious or not suspicious, and employs a mixture of threats and promises to obtain a suspect's cooperation. Most experienced police officers, especially detectives, become highly competent in their craft, and feel more expert than the judge in assessing whether a person should be suspected of wrongdoing. At any rate, the low visibility of their work permits them to follow their judgments. It has been said that policemen are "situation-oriented" in their decisions, but these are reviewed by judges who are "rule-oriented."

The police administrator's practice in evaluating the performance of individual precincts, squads, detectives, or officers, is to tabulate their rates of "clearance" of crimes by arrest. As a consequence, Skolnick (1966) observed, the police prefer to interpret a reported offense as unfounded if there is little prospect of solving it, and otherwise to link it to some arrest whether or not the arrest can result in a conviction.

Both those who believe that police are justified in following their own judgment when stopping people whom they perceive as suspicious, and those who criticize this practice can find support for their separate views from figures obtained by Black and Reiss (1967). These come from systematic observations of over eleven thousand police encounters with citizens in high crime districts of Boston, Chicago, and Washington, D.C., recorded by thirty-six observers working in randomly distributed time periods around the clock for seven days a week, in seven weeks of the summer of 1966. They found that the police only infrequently asked permission to search or to interrogate, but subjects rarely objected to police doing this. One-fifth of the "frisks" of persons yielded a dangerous weapon, and one-half of the property searches produced something that the subject did not want the police to find. Of 131 admissions of guilt made to the police, about half were given before the police began their questioning, and 20 percent were made immediately after questioning began. One may presume this was because those who were guilty knew that they were caught, and that there was an availability of witnesses or evidence. An astute lawyer at their side, however, might have obstructed justice by advising them not to confess, and subsequently so delayed witness and evidence presentation as to get some of them off without being charged, or to get them dismissed in court. Some, of course, may still have achieved this for the accused after admissions to the police. In only 6 percent of the encounters with citizens did the police behave in a negative or hostile manner, whereas citizen behavior to the police was hostile in about twice that proportion of the transactions (Black and Reiss, 1967; Reiss, 1968; Bordua and Reiss, 1967, pp. 295–298).

Because police are concerned with maintenance of public support, they are highly responsive to public pressures on the kinds of services they visibly provide. The statement that the public gets the police service it deserves is basically correct because it tends to receive the police service it demands. The police are especially responsive to influential politicians, but these reflect articulate interest groups and their assessment of predominant public views. The police are not responsive to the public, however, in regard to committing abuses invisible to the public, or about which the public is apathetic.

The absolute power of the police in a private situation and the low status of most offenders with whom they deal encourage abuse. There are norms of secrecy among police officers for fear that any criticism of one policeman may hurt all, so even a police officer who is corrupt or a sadist may not be disciplined or discharged (Westley, 1953, 1956; Stoddard, 1968). The partner system of police patrol creates a high degree of mutual dependence between officers, and encourages their norm of not informing on one other. The practice of most police chiefs of adamantly refusing to criticize their officers to the mass media, even when confronted with photos and multiple witnesses of unwarranted violence by the police, reflects this norm. It may be necessary for the chiefs' support by their men, but it often discredits the police to the public.

James Q. Wilson, from an intensive study of diverse police systems, suggested that there are three major styles of policing in the United States (1968). The still-surviving oldest pattern is what he calls the *watchman* style. It was traditional in cities where police appointment was controled by political machines which were closely linked with organized crime. Such police forces have a low rate of action in illegal selling or consumption offenses, as well as in most illegal performances, petty theft and juvenile delinquency. The officers receive low pay and low rates of promotion, have little education or training, and are recruited locally. Often a share in the payoffs from organized selling augments their income. A consequence is a police service in which high status people get law enforcement against predations, and low status individuals get minimum effort. The police provide peacekeeping services and watch for serious crime, but take little initiative with respect to it.

At the opposite extreme is the *legalistic* style of policing, frequent in areas where the police force is very modern because population has grown rapidly, as in the western states. There the police recruit nationally, require a minimum of high school, and often some college education, have an internal investigating unit on police malpractices, and emphasize the fullest possible enforcement of the law. They tend to treat alike all those who clearly violate the law by seeking penalties in the court, although their policies seem prejudicial because their patrols are most extensive and aggressive in lower status areas.

Wilson calls a third style of policing, which seems to be growing, the *service* approach. It is especially common in some of the larger new suburbs, or in those sheriff's police which have contractual arrangements to police in many suburban towns. They emphasize courtesy and community relations with their predominantly middleclass population. They crack down vigorously on felonies, particularly by outsiders, but tolerate the vices of residents. They usually have high salaries and emphasize appearance and neatness in recruiting officers. They are oriented to maintaining public support, especially where there is an elected sheriff, by trying to minimize complaints and maximize goodwill.

Those recommendations of President Johnson's Commission on Law Enforcement and the Administration of Justice that have been carried out under the Nixon Administration are primarily in regard to police. Expenditures under the Omnibus Crime Control bill were mainly to transform police forces from the watchman to the legalistic style, although some growth of the service style is also evident. Federal grants have subsidized more police training, improved equipment, and brought about more specialized staff components. But despite more efficiency from these measures, animosity towards the police appears to have grown in large segments of the public. It has been provoked by police conflict, first with minority groups seeking civil rights, and subsequently with students and others protesting America's military involvement in Indo-China.

Police-Public Relationships

Studies show that police work tends to make officers feel isolated from the community. In Britain two-thirds said that they felt isolated, and the majority said that the public seemed guarded in their presence (Morton-Williams, 1962). In a more limited American sample, 40 percent of the police said that their work made them feel isolated and 35 percent said that it also made their families feel isolated (Clark, 1965). Surveys indicate, however, that in both Britain and the United States the public is predominantly favorably inclined towards the police, even in the minority groups (Morton-Williams, 1962; President's Commission, 1967, p. 99).

A discrepancy between police and public views may be inherent in the fact that the sample of the public with whom the police most often come in contact disproportionately includes those about whom the police have suspicions. Also, the power of the police may arouse self-consciousness in others because most people commit minor law violations at one time or another. Police are inclined to be hostile towards social workers and others whose approach to deviants is less punitively oriented than their own, and they seem to arouse the generalized hostility which many feel towards all authority figures, a hostility especially prevalent among the adolescence recapitulators of all ages with whom the police must frequently deal. Finally, the "working personality" of the police may itself evoke tension in others and result in mutual aloofness. Insofar as the police feel isolated and view the public as hostile, they are made more cohesive, and more likely to think in the "we-versus-they" mentality characteristic of warfare.

Polarization of public opinion regarding government policy towards civil rights and foreign affairs has burdened the police with much more than their normal experience in handling crowds. Unfortunately, much of the so-called expert training for this that the police have received was derived from the military, who are more oriented to coping with reactions of a wartime enemy than with assuring free expression by their fellow citizens. This is aggravated by the traditional and normal police concern with receiving "respect" from people with whom they deal, and by the fact that crowd situations give some demonstrators a sense of license for verbal abuse of authority figures, including those immediately at hand, the police. A purely military tactical approach by the police is sometimes evident in promiscuous shelling of universities and their surrounding neighborhoods with tear gas, no-knock entrance into student housing to arrest residents indiscriminately, and in a few extreme cases, the pouring of massive gunfire into a general area occupied by students. Following such events, the already mentioned police norm of hiding the deviant acts of some of their members from the public, and of chiefs refusing to admit any wrongdoing by their staffs, further aggravate the public.

Solutions to these problems must be diverse. Effective methods for preventing conflict, well-developed in New York City, are to train police to handle public demonstrations by cooperating in planning them, using marshals from among the demonstrators to help control other demonstrators, tolerating abuse which is purely verbal, and exhibiting a general permissiveness towards expression of nonviolent dissent. The task of the police should be to facilitate, not to frustrate, any expression of dissent that is nonviolent. Unnecessary restrictions, prodding, unwarranted curfews, rigid time limits on public gatherings, and dragnet arrests only divert demonstrator energy away from orderly dissent communication, and increase the probability of violence.

The problem of discipline for misbehaving officers has been a source of heated controversy. The proposal which police have resisted most vigorously is that of civilian review boards to whom complaints might be addressed by the public. The police would prefer to handle their own internal violations by secret disciplinary boards. Legalistic police forces have internal investigation units that act upon complaints and even try to entrap officers suspected of corruption by posing as civilians and offering them bribes. Persons aggrieved by the police, however, are often reluctant to bring their complaints to police agencies; many police staff are certainly biased in assessing complaints about the police, and even if they are not, the credibility of their claims to nonbias will be questioned because they operate secretly and are part of the police organization. An institutionalized Ombudsman office to receive and investigate complaints on all components of government is firmly established in Scandinavia and New Zealand, and has been proposed here. It has the greatest promise of all grievance processing arrangements, although its effectiveness would be more limited in dealing with police actions involving clear violation of official directive than it would be in dealing with acts of the discretionary overlooking of offenses, or matters not covered by law or regulation (Herman Goldstein, 1967).

A problem that will persist even when public opinion on political issues is less polarized and demonstrations are infrequent is that of discretionary enforcement of the law. Somewhat opposing positions have been taken by two prominent commentators, each named Goldstein, on this problem. Both have based their positions on analyses of the American Bar survey studies (e.g., LaFave, 1965). Professor Joseph Goldstein of Yale Law School has vigorously argued for full enforcement. His contention (1960) is that "the police should not be delegated discretion not to invoke the law," for this usurps the legislature's power to determine what behavior should be punished, and makes police conduct not subject to review, for there is no record of nonenforcement. A law that cannot be enforced should be recognized as such and repealed, but other laws should be enforced fully if we are to realize the democratic process in lawmaking and the ideal of equality before the law.

Herman Goldstein, cited earlier, is a political scientist on the faculty of University of Wisconsin Law School, who is experienced in police administration. He calls for explicit recognition of a policy of discretion (1963). His arguments include (in paraphrase):

1. The police can best deal with public demands for law enforcement if they are not always on the defensive about the necessity for discretion, but indicate specifically the magnitude of resources needed for the responsibilities given them.
2. Pressure can then be placed on proponents of new laws to consider their enforceability before passing them, and the police, as experts on enforce-

ability, should be articulate on the enforcement burdens involved in proposed legislation.
3. Public support is greatly increased in regard to many offenses if the police do not enforce the law unless there is noncooperation after a warning is given, as is often done in negligence offenses (e.g., an officer making a driver pull into a gas station to have defective car lights fixed, rather than giving him a ticket because of them).

Herman Goldstein indicates that the choice is not between full enforcement or none, but a more complex choice of the most effective use of resources for increasing conformity to the law.

Still another approach to encouraging police discretion emphasizes the benefits offered by diversion from judicial trial and official punishment for some criminal careers. This is especially stressed with juveniles, where police referral to responsible family members or social work agencies is preferred to arrest as an initial reaction in most cases. As indicated previously, illegal performance and even predations that are a consequence of addictions may be more adequately treated by medical than by punitive measures. New procedures for adult misdemeanants which involve a neighborhood social service office for those not barred as multiple offenders uncooperative in social service has been proposed in Connecticut as an alternative to judicial trial (Price, 1968). All these measures are also justified as reducing the work of police and courts to give them more time for other functions.

One measure for improving police communication with the public is to assign permanently a small number of officers and vehicles to a limited area of the city, smaller than the usual precinct, instead of having them cruise a wider area and rotate assignments. This would increase personal acquaintance between police and residents. The Area Team would be composed of detectives, youth officers, patrolmen, and community relations specialists (Bordua, 1968). This was approximated in 1970 in Los Angeles with the Basic Car Plan, whereby the nine officers required to man one police vehicle twenty-four hours a day seven days per week are assigned a limited number of blocks and monthly meetings are organized to increase communication between them and the area residents. Initial trials in a few areas were considered highly successful, and the practice was greatly extended. The major risk involved is that familiarity fosters corruption, but this is apparently viewed as a lesser risk than unfamiliarity, which promotes hostility.

Perhaps the greatest potential contribution of the President's Commission to resolving police-public problems is its pioneering in survey research (1967, Chapter 2). The Commission sponsored inquiries in high crime-rate areas of three cities and also on a national basis in which representative samples of the public were asked: (1) if any in their household had, in the past year, been a victim of any of a list of crimes; (2) if so, had they reported the offenses to the police; (3) if not, why not; (4) if so, how satisfied were they with the police reactions; (5) had they ever been stopped by the police for questioning. Additional questions were asked regarding their fear of crime and their general attitudes towards the police. These pinpointed the segments of the population which were least satisfied with the police, the basis for their dissatisfaction, and the amount of crime not reported to the police. If such surveys were regularly conducted in all communities by professional survey research agencies, with the results provided to the police and the public, there could be much more rational guidance of both police practice and legislative policy, and a much more realistic awareness of the sources of both accord and tension. It would probably move all police closer to the service style, which is optimum for police-public relationships.

The remaining issue to be raised in this chapter, that of police compliance to constitutional dictates on procedure, is best presented in conjunction with a discussion of the courts as regulators of police legality.

Chapter **5**

THE COURTS

The state's role in dealing with crime began with attempts to settle private feuds, in which a person who considered himself the victim of predation fought those who had allegedly victimized him. Friends and relatives joined in, each side preying on the other; but this was so disruptive to society that private quarrels of all sorts were increasingly made public concerns. Major predations were declared crimes against the state as well as the victim. All societies sufficiently complex to have a monetary system seem to require judicial agencies to settle disputes (Freeman and Winch, 1957). The types of predation subject to penalty by the state increase as economic institutions become more complex (Hall, 1952).

Because feelings are so intense in feuds, an effort is often made to promote compliance with judicial edicts by presenting them as based on superhuman wisdom and authority. In medieval Europe mystical beliefs were invoked, by which the accused were given ordeals by fire or other torture with faith that God would spare the innocent. Today the black robes, elevated bench, and pomp and ceremony in judicial performance still seem designed to convey the impression that the judge is somehow apart from and above the humans before him.

Courts resolve many types of dispute, including those caused by damage claims, breaches of contract, and settlement of estates, in addition to crime. Separate criminal courts have existed in large cities since the

Roman Empire, but in many small communities they still are not separated, although the local court employs a somewhat distinct procedure when handling criminal matters. It is with the criminal courts or criminal procedure that we are here concerned.

Two types of criminal procedure evolved in Europe. The *inquisitorial* prevails on the Continent. Here the prosecutor and a judge collect pretrial evidence and testimony from all concerned parties, separately and in secret, before making a public accusation. The judge then hears the evidence and argument with much more control over how it is presented than occurs in the United States. He actively directs questions to lawyers of both sides. Important cases may be heard by a board of judges, or by a mixed panel of both judges and laymen, but the latter are of above average qualifications.

In Britain and the United States, and in other countries deriving their law from the British, the *accusatorial* or *adversary* procedure prevails. Here the trial is a kind of sham battle between lawyers for the accused and for the state, with the judge serving as an umpire to see that they fight fairly rather than conducting the inquiry. When the battle is over he decides who has won; but if the defense prefers, it may elect in advance to have a jury of twelve laymen decide this instead of the judge. In the United States only a small percentage of criminal cases employ juries.

It should be stressed that the foregoing is a somewhat idealized account of these two systems, intended to emphasize their most contrasting features. Each has many variations in different nations or provinces, and in our fifty-one state and federal judicial systems. To some extent the two systems are changing and becoming similar, as courts of all nations now mix inquisitorial and accusatorial methods.

A striking development in our criminal procedure, especially in large cities, is that the adversaries usually negotiate out of court or interrupt the trials for informal negotiations, sometimes with the judge as participant, and they thereby reach an understanding on how to reduce or eliminate their differences before the trial is concluded. In some cities 95 percent of trials end by an agreement of the prosecution to accept a plea of guilty under negotiated conditions, such as dropping some charges if the accused pleads guilty to others, instead of letting a judge or a jury decide if the accused is guilty (Newman, 1966).

To understand why this "negotiated justice" has developed and to comprehend other features of our courts, one must again consider the four concerns introduced in discussing the police: *selection, efficiency, fairness* and *system maintenance*. However, these are more confounded in the courts, because several somewhat autonomous parties—the judge, the prosecutor, and the defense—pursue these concerns independently of each other. Furthermore, the impact of these factors differs during each of the several separate phases of criminal procedure. It is probably best to discuss major phases posing unique policy issues separately before attempting to generalize on court operations as a whole. The phases are differentiated by the issues and rights they pose rather than by traditional labels for procedural stages, although these also are indicated.

Arrest and the Right to a Hearing

When a person is arrested, the police are required to bring him before a judge without "unnecessary delay." Usually this is within twenty-four hours. The right of *habeas corpus* in our legal tradition is designed to assure a prompt hearing in court if one is arrested. When anyone is held without being properly brought before a judge in a reasonable amount of time, a note to this effect—the *writ of habeas corpus*—can be submitted to any judge in the area. He is required to give such writs first priority, and to give the subject a hearing if he finds this has been denied. The purpose of the initial appearance before a judge is to obtain his decision on whether the police had "probable cause" for the arrest. If the judge finds that police do not indicate reasonable grounds to justify the arrest, he can order the charges dropped and the accused released.

When the police make an arrest they are expected to write the name of the accused, the time and place of arrest, and the charge on a form which is submitted to the most convenient and appropriate court, often that of a magistrate in the same building as the police station. Sometimes the police wish to detain someone for questioning, or wish to prevent his fleeing, or his coaching or intimidating witnesses, before they complete enough of their investigation to be able to present "probable cause" for arrest. It is in such cases that a writ is appropriate, and vocational predators or illegal sellers will often arrange to have a lawyer promptly obtain their release by writ. Usually, however, suspects come voluntarily to a police station if requested to do so, as they know—or are informally advised—that their chances for leniency are best if they are cooperative.

If an arrest is made on a warrant issued by a judge, the *habeas corpus* writ is inappropriate, except when the legality of the warrant is challenged. The police may also issue the accused a summons to appear in court at a specified time, without arresting him, a practice most common in traffic offenses.

Initial Appearance: Right to Counsel

It is at the initial appearances in court, before trial begins, that the rights guaranteed by the Supreme Court decisions of the 1960s have their major impact. In the first place, the accused has a right to counsel. The police or the jailer are expected to allow him at least one phone call after his arrest, which may be used to call a lawyer or to call a friend or relative and ask him to seek a lawyer. Liberal use of the telephone when arrested, to call several people if necessary, seems reasonable to most arrestees and their friends, but is seldom permitted.

When the accused does not have counsel, he has the right to have the court appoint one for him. In some states he must swear that he cannot afford a lawyer before being offered a court-appointed lawyer for no fee. Where the offenses are minor, he may usually waive right to counsel. In petty crimes use of lawyers is the exception rather than the rule. In serious crimes, however, the accused may have a difficult time persuading the court that he does not need counsel, for there is much wisdom in the maxim: "A man who is his own lawyer has a fool for a client."

In most cases where the charge is serious and the accused cannot afford a lawyer, defense counsel is appointed by the court. There are several ways of doing this. In some states a Public Defender's office with a staff of lawyers to serve all who face criminal charges is supported by the county. In other states judges appoint lawyers for the indigent from those attorneys who indicate that they are available for this work, and these lawyers receive a standard fee from the state or county (for example, fifty dollars per case). Formerly, a Legal Aid Society or a special committee of the local bar association arranged voluntary legal services for the indigent, but this is becoming less frequent as the right to counsel is more widely enforced. Only a handful of lawyers specialize in defending criminal cases for a fee, sometimes no more than six or eight in a large city, because there are few criminals who can afford to pay fees competitive with what lawyers can expect for a given amount of effort, usually in more attractive settings, in noncriminal law practice (e.g., divorces, contracts, taxes, estates).

If a case is protracted there may be a change in lawyers one or more times. For indigents, courts readily appoint a new lawyer to take on a case, often with only a few minutes of preparation, if the original appointee is not available. Wealthier defendants may dismiss one lawyer and hire another. In major cases, such as a murder trial or one with many codefendants, two or more lawyers may be employed, working as a team.

Many young lawyers are provided by the criminal courts with opportunities for experience and for political and professional contacts. They are employed either as "deputy assistant district attorneys" (in some states called "state's attorneys") or in public defender service (sometimes called "legal aid"). In metropolitan counties these will be large staffs, with a few senior lawyers in supervisory positions who participate in court activities only for major cases. Since they all work in the same building day after day, defense and prosecution lawyers come to know each other well, in addition to having some acquaintance with the judges and with the few private lawyers specializing in criminal defense. When cast on different sides in the hearings, each could make the work of the other more frustrating or more rewarding in terms of effort required and results obtained, but there usually evolves in every case a series of compromises to maximize the extent to which both sides are satisfied.

The prosecution is interested in selecting those cases for which it can obtain a conviction on some charge, and in having a low percentage of acquittals to report to the voters at election time. The defense is interested in being of some service to their clients, but not necessarily in getting them off completely if they are, in fact, guilty. Each can help the other achieve these separate objectives efficiently in the several phases of the judicial process—most of which are pretrial—which will be described.

Any lawyer who operates according to the informal understandings within the range of give and take considered appropriate is approved in courthouse social circles; if not, he finds collegial relationships less pleasant, and before long he either conforms or seeks other places of employment.

Initial Appearance: Confirmation of Arrest

Once the judge is satisfied as to availability of counsel, he hears the testimony of the arresting officers, which in a serious matter is presented under the direction of the lawyer for the prosecution.

The defense attorney can question the officers and can present objections to their testimony. For example, if their justification for the arrest is material evidence obtained in a search, the defense may ask whether there were legal grounds for the search, such as a warrant, or probable cause for arrest preceding search of the person and his vehicle or immediate surroundings. He may question the connection of the evidence, such as stolen goods or narcotics, with the defendant, perhaps asking how the police know these items were not left at the defendant's house by someone else if the defendant claims he did not put them there. If a confession by the accused is claimed, he may deny having made it, or can retract by claiming he made it under duress. The defense can question whether the accused was properly warned that he need not answer, or informed of his right to have counsel when interrogated by the police. If witnesses are reported, defense counsel can question whether they were in a position to see the offense, or he can question their competence.

At this stage witnesses are not in court and the evidence may not be there; the police are merely reporting what they can present in a trial, if necessary, and both the defense and the judge may question them. The court need not establish guilt beyond a reasonable doubt at this time, only that there appears to be adequate grounds for arrest and trial.

Since the Supreme Court decisions of the 1960s, the initial appearance has been a more demanding experience for the police, since there are now more grounds on which they can be questioned and their charges dismissed. In some courts one can regularly see many defendants brought in for alleged possession of marijuana, gambling material, or stolen goods, who are dismissed because the search was made illegally, or because the police cannot prove that the defendant was the only one who could have placed these goods where they were found. Often the police field procedure is proper, but their way of describing it when testifying or when answering defense attorney questions creates doubt as to their probable cause when they made the arrest, so the charges are dismissed.

It should be noted that the sophisticated offender is aware of the legal technicalities which may free him, and may tell complete lies persuasively to his lawyer, even concocting false stories about police behavior. The police must present rebuttal evidence, or convince the court of their ability to do so at a later hearing. Sometimes the judge must make a decision purely on the basis of which of two conflicting accounts he deems most credible, with serious doubts resolved in favor of the accused.

When the judge dismisses charges and orders the accused freed, he may lecture the police on their improper procedure, possibly also warning the defendant not to be involved in such suspicious circumstances again— but in any case, humiliating the police. Occasionally the police expect their charges to be dismissed, but follow the directives of their supervisors in making arrest just to harass suspected persons whom they cannot easily convict (usually illegal sellers), but whom they can repeatedly arrest and hold until their dismissal in court the next day—hoping thus to deter their coming to that police district. Some judges neither humiliate the police nor inform them as to the reasons for dismissing charges, leaving police to blame dismissal of their cases entirely on the judge. (Of course, they may be inclined to blame the judge even if he does offer a full explanation, it being human nature to blame others instead of oneself.) Officers may also be somewhat indifferent about the outcome of court hearings because they meet the customary police work standard in coping with crime, which, as indicated in the last chapter, is only whether it is cleared by arrest.

The judge, in dismissing cases when he believes the arrest or charges are based upon improper police procedure, often sees himself as educating the police. Defense lawyers also frequently give this justification when criticized because they use irregularities of arrest or interrogation procedures as a basis for obtaining dismissal of charges against persons whom they know are guilty. Legal norms expressed in the Bill of Rights only gain precision and uniformity of implication, however, if ruled upon in specific cases by courts at all levels. But because each case is somewhat unique, lawyers often disagree as to whether a higher court's ruling in another case applies to the case at hand. In a multi-judge court there may properly be a diversity of opinion among different judges, which certainly makes it difficult for the police to be instructed by judicial action. A second difficulty is that communication in a situation humiliating to an officer is not an effective technique of pedagogy. Thirdly, the judge's communication does not reach the entire police force when he addresses only one or two officers at a time, and these are usually not in a supervisory position.

After reviewing these problems, Herman Goldstein (1968) discusses a number of possible remedies for them. One is to have the judges systematically instruct the police, but this often conflicts with a judge's notion of his impartiality; he would feel equally obliged to instruct the defense. Another is for judges to communicate their objections to police testimony to the prosecutor, and have him coach the police. To some extent the deputy assistant prosecutors coach the police in reviewing with them in advance the testimony they expect to present in a particular case. The senior state or district attorney is an elected county official, however, and usually hopes to run for a higher office at the next election, as few seek careers as chief prosecutors. He is not inclined to undertake a task not assigned to his office, such as the systematic education of all police in his county, most of whom are either in autonomous municipal governments or under a separately elected sheriff, possibly of a different political party. Besides, the elected state or district attorney is not informed on details of testimony in any but the most publicized cases; he leaves most cases to his staff, and he is involved in much noncriminal legal work as attorney to the county.

A third solution is to have the judiciary as a whole prepare a set of rules covering their most frequent problems with police testimony. This has been done in Britain but only minimally. It has merit, but cannot anticipate all problems, since cases are so diverse. Therefore, a more continuous system of effective communication is needed. Informal conferences might be of some benefit, but the fear of partiality may still inhibit judges from stating in advance what sort of testimony they desire for specific types of situations.

Goldstein's final suggestion, also tested successfully in Britain, is to provide lower court judges with clerical staff to facilitate their preparing written statements to the police administration whenever they find the behavior of police officers in a case legally objectionable. This might encourage more deliberate and consistent rulings by the judges, and more effective training and supervision of police to promote compliance with judicial expectations.

This "written accountability" policy has not been adopted, however, and if adopted it would probably often be honored with only vague and perfunctory communications, because it would not eliminate the basic cause of poor coordination between judicial activities and operations of the police or corrections. This cause is simply that these agencies do not form one system for the administration of justice; they are separate and nearly autonomous systems with the incentives which influence policy in one often not affecting the other.

This noncoordination of incentives can be illustrated by many observations. One is the scheduling of lower court hearings. The judges are autonomous in this activity and it is customary for them to schedule all those to be heard on a given day for the hour when the day's 'hearings begin, for example, at 9 or 10 A.M. All police officers, defendants, witnesses, relatives, and lawyers must then be available at the opening of court, not knowing whether they will be called immediately or be kept waiting all day, usually on very uncomfortable benches in crowded courtrooms. Some approximate schedule is often communicated to lawyers and police, but it is extremely imprecise, and results in much waste of their time. What has occurred is that the hearing schedule is designed to maximize the efficiency of the judge with minimal concern for the interests in efficiency of police, prosecutors, or defense attorneys.

Another illustration of the nonsystem character of the administration of justice in the United States, already indicated, is the police reliance on clearance by arrest as their criterion of effectiveness. Although the basic assumption of our criminal law is that a person is arrested to secure his conviction, the police make no systematic effort to assess their effectiveness from this standpoint. It is administratively simplest for them to evaluate and to terminate their work on a case with the arrests of all those whom they think are guilty, but the significance of their arrests for society is quite different according to whether the court dismisses the arrestees at their initial appearance, or convicts and sentences them.

Because the time lapse between initial court appearance in a criminal case and its final disposition by a judicial ruling is difficult to predict, the task of compiling statistics on the court consequences of police arrests is administratively complex. Nevertheless, with modern machine records and computer tabulation of data, a police statistician working with the courts could compile conviction rates fairly well as of a year after arrest. He could make separate tabulations for the force as a whole and for its different components, as well as for various types of offense or offender, and for the separate courts. This is not done, however, because the police and the courts each operate as separate self-evaluating agencies, neglecting what in fact is the major consequence of their actions for society—how they affect each other's activities, and that of corrections. Optimally the statistical evaluation of all administration of justice operations—by police, courts, or corrections—should be in terms of their effects on the crime rate and on the careers of offenders.

Initial or Subsequent Appearances: Bail-Setting

If the judge finds that there is probable cause for arrest, he must decide whether trial will proceed immediately, and if not, whether the accused should be confined pending trial. Either the prosecution or the defense may object to an immediate trial in order to prepare their case, and if the charge is serious the judge is not permitted to try it immediately, even when all parties are ready for trial.

When there is a delay, the judge must schedule the next court appearance in the case and decide what should be done with the accused until then. The alternatives include: (1) "remanding" him to custody of the sheriff for confinement in jail; (2) "release on recognizance," which is accepting his promise that if freed he will be in court at the time scheduled; (3) release on bail bond. The latter is a practice whereby the accused deposits a sum of money or title to an equivalent amount of property, on agreement that he forfeits this if he does not appear in court. Bonding companies have developed which offer to pledge this money for the accused for a fee. An understanding of "the bail problem" in the United States will be a good introduction to the influence of the private interests of court personnel in determining judicial procedures.

In the United States, judges and prosecutors are elected. A prosecutor's position is prominent and is frequently a stepping-stone to higher office; many governors and a few presidents have been former prosecutors. The prosecutor's office has a fairly large staff whose appointment he controls, so he has patronage jobs to allot. Judicial office is also attractive to lawyers, and many make great efforts to obtain a party's nomination. Campaigning for election requires large sums of money and the service of numerous volunteers, to many of whom the election winner is obligated when awarding jobs and other favors. Bail bondsmen have traditionally been large contributors to political campaigns, in exchange for which they may expect bail to be set high.

There are many ramifications to the bonding enterprise. For example, although bondsmen must be licensed by the state and are supposed to have sufficient capital to cover the bail they pledge, frequently they do not have the capital and often the bonds are not forfeited—even when the accused does not appear in court when his next hearing is scheduled, and has no reasonable excuse (e.g., illness). Furthermore, when persons fail to appear, or when the bondsman has reason to believe that they will depart the area and not appear, he may take them into custody himself, bring them to the jail and cancel the bonding pledge. There is little judicial control over his arrest procedures in this purely private policing action.

In crowded city courts particularly, bail tends to be automatically set at a specified amount for each type of charge. For example, it will be fixed at five thousand dollars for a felony, with still higher sums for armed robbery. The Eighth Amendment to the U.S. Constitution directs that "excessive bail shall not be required." This has been interpreted as giving everyone a right to release "on reasonable bail" until proven guilty, and sometimes even after that, while the conviction is appealed to a higher court. Capital offenses, primarily murder, are the only ones in which bail of any amount may be denied.

While the purpose of bail is to assure the offender's appearance in court, the practice is to set bail automatically according to the offense, rather than the evidence on the probability of the offender's taking flight to avoid trial. Flight is often more a function of the character of the individual than of the offense with which he is charged; but the offense charged is specific, while character is difficult for a lawyer to demonstrate quickly and conclusively at a hearing on bail. Nevertheless, it is usually recognized that a person with no roots in the community and a long criminal record may be more likely to flee after arrest on a particular charge than a person who has long residence, employment and family ties in the community. Also, a vocational or addiction-supporting predator often sees no alternative but to commit further crimes when out on bail, while an avocational offender ceases crime. Cost of bail or lawyer may also motivate adolescent recapitulators or other impulsive criminals to further predations. Sometimes the judge knows such criminal career information and takes it into account, but in big cities this is infrequent, and bail is set impersonally by the offense charged. Indeed, police are often authorized to release arrestees on *station house bail,* prior to court appearance, if the offense is minor, charging a sum fixed by court rule for each type of crime.

Because bail is determined by the offenses charged, it is inflated initially, for prosecutors encourage police to make as many separate charges and the most extreme charges that are at all reasonable. This practice permits bargaining later for reduction of charges in exchange for pleas of guilty to the lesser charges. The severe charges, however, increase the bail.

The ordinary person cannot immediately post five or ten thousand dollars bail, which may be necessary in a felony case. This has resulted in the bonding business, in which bondsmen pledge the bail for a fee. They are licensed by the state, and are a type of insurance firm. The fees of bondsmen are typically ten dollars for the first hundred dollars and five dollars for each additional hundred dollars. The only way most people can obtain pretrial release is to have their families deliver such a sum to the bondsman, which they do not recover. About two-thirds of those arrested, however, fail to make bond and are held in jail. Sometimes release on bond occurs after the accused has been in jail for some days or weeks, because of the time required for his family to raise the bond or for his lawyer to negotiate reduction of charges or of bail, or both.

Police are often alleged to arrest persons whom they suspect of crime—or against whom they are simply prejudiced—even if there are inadequate grounds for conviction. The police anticipate that the arrestees will be released in court, but will be deterred from offending the police again or even coming into the same police district because the arrest results in their being jailed or being released on payment of a bonding fee which they forfeit. Recovery of bonding costs in cases of arrest leading to dismissal of charges, and even monetary compensation for such arrests, has been proposed as an equitable restitution for damages suffered from state employees, and as a policy that would discourage improper or unwarranted arrests.

The most influential development in American bail history began in New York City in 1962 when the Vera Foundation, a private organization, established the Manhattan Bail Project. A judge agreed to have New York University law students interview pretrial prisoners on factors believed indicative of their not fleeing to avoid trial. The students assigned a specified number of points to a prisoner for each favorable characteristic, such as stability of employment, marriage, children, an honorable military service record, and no prior criminal record. Interview responses of the prisoners were checked by phone calls. A randomly selected half of those with scores on these items totalling above a certain minimum were then recommended for release on recognizance rather than bail. This procedure proved strikingly effective, with 98.4 percent of those released on recognizance appearing for trial compared to 97.0 of those in the control group who posted bail. The New York City Probation Department has since established a separate unit purely for checking on qualifications for release on recognizance. The practice has spread to over a hundred jurisdictions, though usually not on as extensive a scale as in New York, because of lobbying against it by bondsmen.

An alternative bail reform introduced in Illinois in 1964 consists of socializing the bail business. The state charges only 10 percent of the bail set, somewhat more than what the bondsmen charge, but 90 percent of this is returned to the accused when he appears for trial. The 10 percent of the 10 percent retained covers administrative costs of the system. Essentially, the state recognized the bail bond business as an unnecessary burden on the income of the poor.

An additional way of avoiding pretrial confinement is simply to give the accused a summons to appear in court at a certain time, and not even arrest him. This is done for 80 percent of nontraffic offenses in Britain, but until recently, for less than 1 percent in the United States. That summons could be used in lieu of arrest for more cases in this country was shown by the Vera Foundation in the Manhattan Summons Project. In New York City police stations where this was first tried for two years, over one thousand arrestees were experimentally released by the police with a summons to appear in court, and 97.5 percent showed up. This practice has, therefore, been increasing, but quite slowly in most parts of the country.

The third major innovation in pretrial release of the Vera Foundation (with Ford Foundation assistance) is that of pretrial employment for misdemeanants. Those whose employment record is too unstable to make them eligible for release on recognizance, and who cannot make bail, are released on condition that they report regularly during the pretrial period to a vocational training and employment center. It is the responsibility of those operating the center to try to place the releasees in existing public programs of skill training, many paying stipends to trainees, and to get them regular employment at jobs for which they become qualified. The center reports to the court on the releasee's record in these programs, and for those whose cooperation and vocational advancement is good, the judge often dismisses charges or grants probation; without these services these men would not have been good risks for probation and would probably have been sentenced to jail terms, in addition to being jailed while awaiting trial. For many of these releasees there would not have been participation in such public programs if it were not stipulated as a condition for their pretrial release, for many do not know of the programs or have been so frightened or humiliated in dealing with public agencies that they are fearful of initiating transactions for services to which they are entitled.

Continuances

One argument for bail reform is that a larger proportion of persons released pretrial than of persons held in jail are dismissed or acquitted. Also, a larger percentage of convicted persons released pretrial than of those convicted while jailed are given probation (Zeizel, 1969, pp. 627 ff.). This suggests that judges are biased against persons in jail. Statistically speaking, there may be some justification for such bias because: (1) being out for a long time on bail or recognizance without rearrest is a crude test of risk in release on probation, especially if the pre-sentence report shows regular employment while released; (2) factors that make for low commitment to crime, such as employment or family ties, are qualifications for both recognizance and probation, and they are probably correlated with ability to pay bail. More important than this, however, is that a person in jail is motivated to get his trial concluded, so he can start serving his sentence and get out. He more readily pleads guilty. A person out on bail or recognizance is motivated to delay trial as much as he can because the prosecution's case gets "cold" as witnesses scatter or their memories become hazy, the prosecutor becomes more agreeable to reducing the charges "to get it over with" if the accused will plead guilty, and the crime does not look so bad to judge or jury when it is in the more distant past and the accused has been in the community. These factors result in delays of criminal proceedings, which are the concern of this section.

Continuance is the legal term for a postponement of court proceedings. It is authorized by the presiding judge on his own initiative, or at the request of either the prosecution or the defense. There are many bona fide reasons for a continuance, such as time needed by a new lawyer to become familiar with a case, to contact witnesses, or to collect evidence. Time is often required for prosecution to prepare items which defense counsel has a right to request, such as a written bill of particulars on the charges, or a list of the witnesses; and the judge may wish time to consider a request for a change of judges or of courts (*venue*), for the suppression of confessions or of illegally seized evidence, or for the separate trial of codefendants (*severance*) (Banfield and Anderson, 1968). Prosecution may also request continuances to collect new evidence or for various other reasons, but is often more restricted especially by statutory time limits for the period between taking an offender into custody and beginning his trial. This limit is often 120 days, but limits are waived if delay is due to continuances requested by defense counsel, or to investigations of mental competency or other special actions ordered by the judge.

Even casual observation of criminal court proceedings soon reveals a fantastic amount of delay due to continuances. A bona fide reason will be given when the continuance is requested, and most judges grant them automatically, even if skeptical of the reason stated. They grant them to prevent conviction of the offender from being reversed on appeal to a higher court, should the appeal point out that the record shows continuance was denied when a bona fide reason was given in requesting it.

It is widely believed that the actual reason for many, if not most, continuances is not that which is stated when requesting the continuance, but an interest in delaying the case. As indicated, prosecution's interest in delay for other than bona fide reasons is most probable when the defendant is confined and refuses to plead guilty to anything. After he suffers in jail for a while, he may cooperate in a guilty plea just to get out, even if it means leaving the jail for the penitentiary (which is usually more readily borne than the jail and may be considered inevitable). Greatest interest in delay, however, is with the defense, for, as indicated, delay usually impedes presentation of witnesses by prosecution, and interest in punishing often wanes as time passes after a crime is committed. Furthermore, an accused who is out of jail often just wishes to defer punishment—even if he knows it is inevitable.

Defense counsel's interest in delay, however, varies according to the method by which he is paid. If assigned by the court, his fee is fixed by the case, modified only in unusual circumstances, so the more rapidly his cases are concluded the more he earns per hour. If a salaried employee of the public defender, his only motivation is the "production standard" of his office. If volunteering his services to legal aid, he receives no monetary compensation but achieves gratification from doing good works or from the experience, and he must balance this against what value he gives to his time. If privately retained, however, his fees are determined mainly by the time he devotes to the case. He is paid a retainer of several hundred dollars in advance for his services, and when he feels he has done enough work for what he has been paid, he asks for an additional retainer in advance. Time is often required for the defendant's family to procure this money, and they will be reluctant to pay it after the case is already decided, especially if the accused is found guilty. The retained counsel, therefore, has an especially great interest in delays, and it is reported that "courthouse regulars" among defense attorneys often know the judges well enough to be able to ask successfully, though off the record, for a delay so they can collect their fee (Blumberg, 1967, pp. 110–115).

Two separate statistical compilations indicate the impact of these differences in motivation of defense counsel. Blumberg (1967) in what he identified only as "Metropolitan Court," asked 724 convicted defendants in which of their successive contacts with counsel it was that they were advised to plead guilty. Among those with assigned counsel, 60 percent said it was on the first contact; among those with legal aid, 49 percent reported it was on the first contact; and among those with privately retained counsel, only 35 percent said it was on the first contact. In a study of 524 defendants in the Cook County (Illinois) Criminal Court, Banfield and Anderson (1968) found that 65 percent of those with public defenders had one to four court appearances, 26 percent had five to eight appearances, 5 percent had nine to twelve appearances, and 4 percent had thirteen or more appearances. Of those with retained counsel, however, only 32 percent had one to four appearances, 30 percent had five to eight appearances, 20 percent had nine to twelve appearances and 18 percent had thirteen or more appearances. The significance of these delays is indicated by the fact that the percentages of those found guilty were: 92 percent for those with one to four appearances, 76 percent for those with five to eight appearances, 69 percent for those with nine to twelve appearances, 63 percent for those with thirteen to sixteen appearances and 48 percent for those with seventeen or more appearances. This statistical relationship of favorable outcome to number of appearances was still evident in cross-tabulations to hold constant the type of counsel, jail or bail, the type of sentence given those found guilty, and numerous other variables.

There is no ready remedy for these differential apparent impacts of continuances on both the fairness and the efficiency of the courts. Records can be kept of the frequency with which different lawyers request continuances, and their reasons for them, as a possible means of exposing and discrediting the worst abusers, but this involves some risk of confusing these lawyers with the most dedicated defenders who may request continuances with exceptional frequency for genuine reasons. Some judges are more daring than others in denying what they believe to be purely dilatory requests for continuance, and when this does not lead to these denials being the basis for reversal of conviction through the appeal process, abuse of continuance rights may diminish in their courts. When one practices criminal law, however, one often studies judges more than statutes. Lawyers can become both astute at knowing the kind of request a judge has difficulty in refusing, and capable of getting their clients tried before the judges whose behavior they can manipulate most successfully.

Preliminary Hearing, Grand Jury, and Indictment or Information

Usually a *misdemeanor* is defined as an offense for which the maximum confinement penalty is one year in jail, and a *felony* as one in which the minimum confinement penalty is a year and a day in prison. (Jails are usually county and prisons state institutions.) If the charge at arrest is a felony and is not reduced to a misdemeanor in the initial appearance, and the judge does not have jurisdiction to try a felony, the next stage may be a preliminary hearing. In some states this also occurs with the more serious or "indictable" misdemeanors.

The purpose of the preliminary hearing is to ascertain that there is probable cause for convicting the accused of a felony. It may include presentation of some witnesses and material evidence not included at the initial appearance. The accused, however, may waive the preliminary hearing.

If the preliminary hearing confirms that there are reasonable grounds to proceed towards trial, the next step is for the judge to have the case "bound over" to the grand jury. This organization consists of twenty-three laymen, usually appointed for a month, but in some places for as long as a year of part-time service. Only sixteen need be present for a quorum and twelve votes, a majority of the twenty-three, are required for decisions. Their task is to assess the prosecutor's justification for accusing someone of a very serious crime. The formal accusation is called an *indictment*.

The grand jury conducts its hearings in secret. It receives information on the accused only from the prosecutor, with neither the accused nor his counsel present. It may even consider indictment against persons not yet arrested. This jury may call witnesses or request a variety of information on its own initiative, but usually does not use such investigatory powers. Its purpose is to guard against the prosecutor making serious charges damaging to a person's reputation when he cannot prove them. It could be especially useful against a vindictive or irresponsible prosecutor. Because the grand juries usually approve almost all of the accusations recommended by the prosecutor, they are frequently called "rubber stamps" and unnecessary delays in the trial process. They have been eliminated in some states, and their functions greatly reduced in others. In many states where grand juries persist, they are preoccupied mainly with study tasks on topics related to county administration.

When the grand jury is abolished or does not handle criminal cases, or when it normally does indict but defendant elects to waive his right to formal accusation by a grand jury, the indictment is replaced by a legal document called an *information* which the prosecution submits directly to the trial court. Both indictment and information describe the place, time, and circumstances in which particular acts in violation of designated statutes are said to have been committed by the accused. They may have one or more separate charges. Their purpose is to tell counsel for the accused what the prosecution intends to prove so argument and evidence can be prepared for defense against it.

The Trial and Trial Jury

Misdemeanors with light penalties are usually tried at the initial appearance, and often with neither prosecution nor defense counsel present. Right to assigned counsel is usually restricted to offenses with possible penalties above some specific minimum, and sometimes it is not available in all pretrial procedure. A trial in felony court and in serious misdemeanors opens with the arraignment, at which the separate charges on the indictment or information are formally read and the accused is required to plead guilty or not guilty to each.

Pleas of guilty save the time, trouble, and uncertainty of a trial, so the prosecution has much interest in encouraging them—and in busy courts the judges share this interest. The prosecution is also helped if the defendant waives preliminary hearing or grand jury. Much of the pretrial negotiation is an effort of the defense to obtain concessions, such as reduction of charges or favorable recommendations on sentencing, in exchange for helping the prosecution accelerate or avoid trial. The plea can be changed to guilty even after trial has begun. As a result of these negotiations, as many as 95 percent of criminal convictions in large city courts are obtained by a guilty plea rather than by trial verdict.

If the defendant pleads not guilty, he has a right to be tried by a jury, but he may also waive this right. The petit or trial jury is a survival from feudal times when semi-autonomous nobility objected to trial by judges, perhaps not of their social status, and appointed by a distant monarch; they wished to be tried by "a jury of their peers"—the local nobility of their own rank. Since the end of the eighteenth century the principle of "equality before the law" has made everyone legally a peer of everyone else, but the jury still tends to have a highly selective membership. Persons previously convicted of felonies are excluded by statute; teachers, preachers, physicians, dentists, and a number of other professions are usually excused on request, by law or custom. These reductions occur before officials compile "venire lists" of prospective jurors and present them to the court.

The "veniremen" from these lists are called to the court in groups appreciably larger than the twelve plus one or two alternates needed for a trial jury. First the judge, and then attorneys for each side, question prospective jurors on their competence to reach an unbiased verdict; those that the judge does not excuse, the attorneys may challenge, with the judge ruling on the challenge; each side may also challenge a fixed number "per-emptorily," without statement of reasons. Jurors usually receive only nominal pay, such as five dollars per day and meals, and sometimes they are "sequestered"—housed in a hotel when not in session—for the duration of the trial. Employers often give staff leave with pay for jury duty, but usually for an upper limit of twenty or thirty days. If a person does not wish to be a juror, he can usually get himself excused or challenged by claiming hardship or bias. As a consequence, the people who seek and are selected for jury duty are disproportionately old and retired, or housewives.

In general, lawyers prefer trial by judge if arguing legal technicalities, and by jury if appealing to sentiment. When laws are unpopular (e.g., those of the 1920s to implement the Prohibition Amendment) or where circumstances of the offense arouse public sympathy for the offender (e.g., a husband shooting his wife's lover), juries often decline to convict even when evidence of law violation is clear. The social function of the jury appears to be primarily to make the law more flexible. Since jury decisions must be unanimous, a few jury members of strong conviction may deter-mine these decisions. Research has shown that the most articulate and influ-ential jurors are those of highest education or social status (Strodtbeck, *et al*, 1957; James, 1959).

One striking feature of American criminal procedure is the great concern with not allowing anything to be said in the trial unless it bears directly on the specific charges in the indictment or information. Nothing can be uttered in the trial about the character of the accused—one can only say whether he did the acts charged, at the time and place specified—unless his good character is used by the defense as an argument that he could not have committed this crime. Also, witnesses cannot answer questions calling for an opinion rather than a report of their sensory observations, unless their qualification to give an expert opinion is first established.

Because of these concerns that testimony be relevant to the charges and to the competence of the witness, a witness is seldom allowed to give extended accounts in his own words; instead he is only questioned— "examined"—by the lawyer who presents him, and cross-examined by the opposing lawyer. This permits lawyers to object to one another's questions before the answers are given, thus preventing use of questions not relevant to the charges, calling for inexpert opinion, or formulated in a leading or prejudicial manner. The lawyers may also object to answers in which a witness volunteers more than he was asked or is competent to say. This procedure contributes to the slowness of American trials. Research has revealed numerous weaknesses in this method of seeking truth, including errors in recall, and distortions from the manner in which questions are asked (Marshall, 1966). Should the judge uphold a lawyer's objection, he may order a question or an answer stricken from the record of the trial, and instruct a jury to ignore it; but of course, once the jurors or judge have heard something they may not actually be able to remove it from their thoughts.

In our adversary system, appeals of trial verdicts to higher courts are limited to questions of legality in procedure, rather than to the assessment of testimony (as can occur in many other countries). As a result of repeated successful appeals on detailed technicalities of procedure, behavior in court became extremely rigid and formal. Many have the impression that this trend has passed its peak and informality is growing, as appeals have been denied where the alleged violations of procedure could not have substantially affected the court's final decision.

The trial concludes with summary speeches from each side. The defense can precede his summary by a motion that the judge dismiss the charges, or direct the jury to render a verdict of not guilty because the prosecution has failed to present evidence of the facts charged in the indictment. This motion is usually denied. If the trial is by jury the judge then instructs the jury on the law relevant to the charges, especially what they must find proven about the acts of the accused for these acts to fit the statutory definition of the crime with which he is charged.

While the trial procedure described here has become familiar to most Americans through portrayal on television and in motion pictures, as already indicated, it is not a familiar sight in American courtrooms, especially in criminal cases. Instead, the outcome of most prosecution is agreed upon out of court, but only after many deliberately delaying continuances in a large proportion of cases, especially when the accused is out on bail or recognizance and has privately retained his lawyer. When the purpose of courtroom procedures is either to delay the trial or to put into effect an agreement already reached, the public activity of the lawyers in the courtroom is in many ways a sham performance.

"Justice delayed is justice denied" expresses a frequent complaint about American trial procedure. This saying is applied especially to civil trials, such as efforts to sue for damages suffered in an accident, where delays of five years are not rare. Delay is equated with injustice in criminal trials primarily by those clamoring to impose penalties on offenders, notably when they have sympathy for the victims, as was widespread after the assassinations of Martin Luther King and Robert F. Kennedy. In most criminal cases, however, the public inclination is to give the accused every benefit of doubt, so defense rights to delay have become relatively sacred. This is justified because it reduces the risk of convicting the innocent, at the same time that it increases the prospect of discharging the guilty as innocent.

Another justification for defense tactics of delay is that the prosecution usually has more resources than the defense for collecting evidence and testimony, so the defense should be given procedural advantages. The ability of resourceful defense to impede efforts at conviction highlights, however, the unfairness of the courts, since lawyers of poorer defendants cannot bargain as long or investigate as expensively as lawyers of wealthy defendants. Poor adolescence recapitulators or avocational predators, therefore, often receive severer penalties for a given type of offense than do vocational predators, and many of the latter repeatedly escape all penalty following arrest.

Conclusion on Courts

If one looks at the judicial system from the four standpoints used for analysis of the police, one finds that courts: (1) do not select wisely or equitably those offenders for whom state action is appropriate; (2) do not reach decisions efficiently; (3) do not conduct criminal procedure fairly; (4) do not maintain public support for themselves. From these standpoints courts may well be the most unsuccessful major institutions in our society.

Numerous court reform measures have been proposed, and some have been adopted more or less widely. In many states judicial appointments have been taken out of politics, under variations of the "Missouri Plan." Here the judge does not have opposition on the ballot in elections subsequent to his initial appointment or election, the voters responding only "yes" or "no" to a question on whether this judge should be retained for an additional term. This greatly reduces the judge's need to campaign, and hence, to be obligated to others for campaign support, as judges are only removed when involved in major scandal or extremely unpopular actions. Measures to take the prosecutor's office out of politics would be a major additional improvement.

A second type of reform is to integrate all state courts into a single administrative hierarchy. When this is not the case, each judge is almost an absolute monarch in his own courtroom—setting his own work load, procedural style and standards—with his carelessness and indifference having few consequences which affect him, since his nomination and election are based only on his contributions of work or money to the party organization; voters are ignorant of his judicial performance. This explains why Blumberg found that two "workhorses" of the nine judges in "Metropolitan Court" tried 65 percent of the court's cases, and six distinct styles of judicial activity were found among the nine (1967, p. 138). While there will never be complete consistency, since judges are human, a marked improvement of performance in many courts is achieved by maintaining statistics on each judge's work and decision patterns, and giving appellate court judges supervision functions over lower level judges, including for extreme cause, a procedure for disciplining or even removing a judge. New Jersey and a few other states, as well as the federal courts, approximate this.

Much more drastic revisions are probably necessary if our courts are to achieve a highly equitable selection of offenders for state sanctions, efficient yet fair trial procedure, and maintenance of support for the administration of justice as a whole. This is unlikely as long as the behavior of judges, prosecutors, and defense is neither rewarded nor punished by its consequences for the administration of justice as a whole.

Selection of cases, as indicated earlier, is a function of court relations with the police; the present judicial method of trying to make the police more lawful only makes them lawless in more of their activity, because it reduces the percentage of cases in which they seek convictions, and these are usually the only cases in which they are questioned in court on the lawfulness of their procedure. This can be corrected only by: (1) judicial communications to the police that are more pedagogical than autonomous reprimands to lower level police staff in scattered separate cases; (2) police assessment of their own performance by convictions achieved in court rather than merely by arrests.

Efficiency and fairness require less viewing of pretrial and trial procedure as a game with each side concerned solely with making points at the other's expense, and more as a collaborative effort to protect society. This first requires the most accurate methods of determining guilt or innocence. Psychological experimentation with new methods of testimony elicitation or assessment, and administrative experimentation with investigatory staff under the judge's control might be beneficial. Also relevant is the increasing inquisitorial tendency in American procedure, such as allowing the judge to examine witnesses when he finds that examination and cross-examination by prosecution and defense leave important questions inadequately answered. The mentality of lawyers is so geared to the game of winning cases that advice and research should be sought from behavioral scientists who are not lawyers, in an effort to design and test procedural innovations. This may well begin in quasi-judicial organizations, such as regulatory agencies and arbitration boards, where procedure is not as rigidly controlled by legislation and tradition as it is in the courts.

The maintenance of the administration of the justice system depends not only on the foregoing, but especially on coordination of sentencing—a stage of criminal court procedure not yet discussed—with correction administration. These two topics, therefore, will be discussed together in the following chapter.

Chapter **6**

CORRECTION

Correction is the custody, care, or other treatment given persons because they are convicted of crime. Three or more organizations—legislatures, courts, and correctional agencies such as prisons and parole boards—share in determining the form and duration of an offender's correctional experience. The relative influence of each of these types of organization in such determinations has had marked variations, historically and geographically, within the United States.

Sentencing Variations

America's revolutionary reaction to the tyranny of royal judges was expressed by the slogan "a government of laws, not men," and by state legislatures formally fixing all sentences entirely by statute, according to the crime. For example, a person found guilty of a crime for which the punishment prescribed by law was five years confinement was automatically sentenced to this penalty. To take variation of circumstances or of offenders into account, statutes later specified increasingly severer punishment on subsequent convictions or distinguished several degrees of an offense with a different penalty for each. Thus, a person could be charged with burglary in the first degree if he entered an occupied dwelling at night to commit a felony, but in the second or third degree if the building was not a dwelling, was unoccupied, or was entered by day.

In the second half of the nineteenth century, American judges in many states gained more discretion when statutes instituted a range of penalties for each offense, such as from one to ten years for first degree burglary. The judge then set a specific sentence within the statutory range for each person found guilty. For example, he might impose only one year on a crisis-vacillating burglar, and ten years on a professional.

Parole, a development primarily of the twentieth century, though initiated earlier (Glaser, 1968), permits an administrative board to release prisoners on a conditional basis before they complete their sentences. In many states, especially in the North, this is done by means of an *indeterminate sentence* which fixes minimum period of confinement before parole eligibility and maximum duration of confinement (e.g., three to ten years for burglary). In some states, notably several of the western ones, statutes fix an *indefinite sentence* of low minimum and life maximum for many felonies (e.g., one year to life for robbery), thus completely transferring determination of imprisonment from judges to parole boards. In other states the judge may fix the minimum before parole eligibility and a maximum for each case within the statutory range; for example, he might give a vocational burglar eight to fifteen years, but an avocational burglar one to three years. In still other states, especially in the South, a *definite sentence* of a specific number of years is imposed for each imprisonment, but statutes make all prisoners eligible for parole after serving a particular fraction of their sentence—usually a third—or a minimum period. (For a fuller discussion of sentencing variations, see Glaser, Cohen, and O'Leary, 1966.)

To a large extent, all variations of legislation and of parole board policy on sentence determination are offset by the bargaining process in court. When statutes specify penalties for each offense, offenders bargain to plead guilty if the charge is limited to one carrying a lesser penalty. Thus, an armed robbery charge may be dropped if the offender pleads guilty to theft, although he held a gun on his victim. If sentences are made highly indefinite by statute, recidivist felons assume that they will not be paroled early, so they bargain for lower maximum penalties—for example they will plead guilty to offenses carrying five- to ten-year sentences rather than to those carrying one to twenty years. If the judge can fix this range he may become involved in the bargaining, unofficially, by tacit agreement to follow prosecution recommendation on sentencing if the offender pleads guilty. (For a fuller analysis see Ohlin and Remington, 1958.)

Common law tradition permits a judge to suspend the carrying out of a sentence for a specified period, to prescribe the offender's behavior in this period, and, for some crimes, to cancel the sentence later if the convicted person has behaved as the judge directed. Formerly this was done only for offenses committed under unusual circumstances. Since the end of the nineteenth century, however, it has evolved into *probation,* whereby an officer of the court (or an approved volunteer) assists and observes the released offender, and reports on him to the court (Glaser, 1968). In many courts this is the most common penalty for first felony convictions, and is frequent for other convictions as well. Today's probation officer also prepares a presentence report on the past conduct, reputation, plans, and other aspects of the character of each person found guilty. The judge waits for this report—often for many days—before pronouncing sentence.

One additional variation on sentencing is the *fine,* or payment of money to the state as punishment for committing an offense. Though traditionally imposed only for petty crimes, it is increasingly recognized as an effective deterrent for diverse avocational offenders. Jail confinement is required, however, of those who cannot pay their fines, usually at a rate such as one day's confinement for each five dollars of fine. This makes the jail a punishment for poverty as well as for crime. Partial reductions of this inequity include installment payment of fines and the Scandinavian solution of fining a person a given number of days' pay for his offense, so the rich pay more than the poor.

Related to the fine is the requirement that the offender make restitution to the victim for the damages suffered. This is usually a condition of probation, and may be paid on an installment basis. It is limited in applicability by the relative poverty of most offenders, but a requirement of some type of restitution, in services if not in money, is increasingly advocated. Also, a growing number of state and national governments have initiated state payment of restitution to some victims of crime when the offender cannot pay.

Correctional Goals and Procedures

Correctional goals may be summarized as revenge, restraint, rehabilitation, and reintegration, in this sequence of emphasis historically, but with two or more of the goals sometimes simultaneously pursued.

1. *Revenge* is the traditional concern of a victim in reaction to predation. As indicated at the beginning of the previous chapter, the state's role in trying and sentencing predators began with efforts to minimize disruption of society from private vengeance-seeking. In arguments for state policy in punishing criminals, five goals can be distinguished. The first is pure revenge—to satisfy the passions of the victims and their supporters. The second is abstract justice—to balance each wrong with a penalty, as a matter of religious or philosophical principle. The third is called *individual deterrence* by lawyers—to make the punished person fear the consequences of

crime. The fourth is *general deterrence*—to make others refrain from crime from fear of its penalties. The fifth is symbolic—to communicate the state's disapproval of certain acts by classifying them as criminal.

None of these motivations to impose punishment has disappeared by any means, but all are less frequently and stridently voiced now than they once were. Secularization of public thought increasingly forces advocates of a penalty to justify it by empirical evidence of its effects on crime rates rather than by purely abstract or emotional argument. The limited evidence available indicates that the certainty of punishment has a larger inverse correlation with crime rates than the severity. Also, punishment is least effective where offenders have a high commitment to their crimes (e.g., addiction-supporting or vocational predation), or where the crime serves expressive rather than instrumental needs (e.g., public intoxication, paranoid assault). (For fuller discussion see Chambliss, 1967.)

2. *Restraint* at first was used only pending trial and determination of sentence. Punishment was then primarily corporal (e.g., lashings), capital, economic (fines or forfeiture of property), or social (banishment or ostracism). Gradually confinement became the preferred penalty in modern times. Workhouses for misdemeanants—especially "sturdy beggars" and vagrants—developed in Europe in the sixteenth century, but imprisonment became the predominant punishment for felons only in the nineteenth century. The United States led this development with the "Pennsylvania System," promoted by the Quakers of that state. They emphasized solitary confinement with only a Bible and permitted prisoners to communicate only with religiously oriented staff and visitors. Its first *penitentiary* opened in 1829, but was soon rivaled by the "Auburn System," pioneered in New York state, which emphasized group labor in silence by day, and solitary confinement at night. The striped suit and lock-step were later Auburn innovations. Alexis DeToqueville was one of many prominent Europeans who came to America to study and report on its controversial prison programs. The Pennsylvania System was most widely adopted in Europe and the Auburn System in the United States.

3. *Rehabilitation* of prisoners by education, vocational training, and counseling received growing emphasis during the twentieth century. This had begun in the late nineteenth century when *reformatories* were initiated as separate prisons for young adults. Until the Great Depression of the 1930s, however, time for educational endeavors was limited by the fact that most prisons exploited their inmates by making them labor hard for little or no compensation. They worked either on government enterprises or on projects for private businesses which paid the state for their labor. When the Depression brought widespread unemployment in the free community, public pressure led to laws highly restricting convict labor, and prison-made goods are still banned from interstate commerce in the United States. Except

in some southern institutions which still have appreciable income from intrastate sale of penal farm products, most prison inmates do not have the equivalent of full-time work. Nevertheless, up to one-fourth are engaged in manufacturing products for state use (institution clothing, office furniture, highway signs, license plates, etc.), with work incentives provided by a few dollars pay per month and reduction of sentence for good behavior. Only with incentive rewards varying tangibly with achievement, and vocational classwork linked with realistic factory conditions, are large gains in work skill made by many in prison. This is most developed in the U.S. federal prisons, partly because they have all federal government agencies, including the armed forces, as a market for their products. (For fuller analysis, see Glaser, 1969).

Prisoners have a close to normal distribution of I.Q. scores, but are predominantly high school or junior high school dropouts. Those with more education are often used as instructors. Employment of staff teachers has increased, however, as inmate teachers are impaired not just by limited training, in most cases, but also by lack of the authority, social distance, and incentives which are normally part of the teacher's role. Other major impediments of prison education are variations in student preparation and motivation for learning. These are most effectively overcome by programmed education, with definite rewards in money, or increments of freedom, or comfort for each lesson unit completed. This has been shown to permit advancement of several grades per year in a correctional setting (McKee, 1968; Cohen, *et al,* 1966). The latter part of the twentieth century has seen a growth in college level education for prisoners, often in conjunction with nearby community colleges.

Follow-up studies of released prisoners indicate that their rates of complete unemployment are about three times the national average and, in addition, their rate of only part-time employment is about twice the national average. These rates are highest among those in the first postrelease weeks, among nonwhites, and among the unmarried (Pownall, 1969). About 90 percent of reported felonies are property predations, so most of the recidivism of releasees may be regarded as a substitute for legitimate employment. Indeed, there is a close relationship between unemployment and recidivism rates. A rational society—in its self-interest—would make major efforts to improve the work experience and qualification of criminals while it confines them, and to assist—even subsidize—their on-the-job training and employment after release.

Concentration of offenders in penal institutions facilitates their sharing criminal ideas and rationalizations, and may estrange them more than ever from noncriminal social circles. This is especially true in county jails, where pretrial confinement and the serving of misdemeanor sentences occur, since these have maximum isolation of inmates from staff and minimum rehabilitation programs. (See Glaser, 1970.)

In prison life, as outside it, behavior reflects the reference groups of the individual, and these vary in stability. Adolescence recapitulators, especially those institutionalized early in life, tend to be highly committed to immediate comfort and status enhancement in prison. This is achieved by skill at manipulation of other offenders and staff, by various methods of deception, domination, or ingratiation. It is less characteristic of both vocational and avocational or crisis-vacillating predators, since they remain oriented to their outside reference groups, although long imprisonment may diminish this identification (Irwin, 1970).

Research in a variety of correctional institutions has indicated that programs emphasizing intensive counseling or psychotherapy and a permissive social climate have opposite effects on different types of prisoners. This was consistently shown in controlled experiments or quasi-experiments at a naval disciplinary barracks (Grant and Grant, 1959), a California correctional institution for older youth offenders (Adams, 1970), and a Massachusetts penitentiary (Carney, 1969). Prisoners with little prior involvement in crime who expressed a desire for counseling and were in these therapeutically oriented programs had lower recidivism rates than similar prisoners in traditional prison programs. Conversely, those prisoners with more prior criminal experience and strong ties to other criminals who were in these therapeutic programs had markedly higher recidivism rates than similar offenders in traditional "firm but fair" prison regimes. Apparently the most criminalistic inmates used the counseling situations primarily to manipulate staff, rationalize their criminality, and avoid the humiliations of traditional prison life, rather than to prepare realistically for the problems they would encounter in pursuing a noncriminal life outside of prison. Contrastingly, those anxious to avoid further crime apparently developed less identification with other criminals in the therapeutic than in the traditional programs, and possibly gained some insight into their problems of adjustment in the postrelease world. Thus, each type of correctional program may have opposite effects, depending on the subjects to whom it is applied. Therefore, if programs are evaluated for a cross-section of offenders without making appropriate differentiations, these opposite effects offset each other and mask the benefits from each program for some subjects.

It is clear that what is needed for effective correction is a so-called prescriptive penology, to make the state's reaction fit the offender's potential for reform. When a person is successful at crime he tends to repeat it until he is caught, but the discomfort, duration of confinement, and type of assistance—if any—necessary to make him cease crime permanently varies tremendously with the person involved and with his social circumstances.

Ultimately, the test of any rehabilitation program is in the community, rather than in the institution. Therefore, the most important developments in twentieth century correction are probably those which provide alternatives to incarceration or facilitate transition from confinement to assured freedom.

4. *Reintegration* of offenders into society after their presumed rehabilitation by prison programs is proclaimed as the goal of parole. More specific claims comprise the manifest or official functions of parole. These are: (1) to make better decisions on the optimum duration of confinement by deferring such decisions so that they may be based upon observation of the offenders in prison rather than just upon impressions conveyed in the courtroom; (2) to assist released prisoners in achieving a law-abiding life; (3) to protect the public by making release from prison conditional, with surveillance of the releasees so that they may be promptly reconfined if they show evidence of not conforming to conventional norms and drifting back into crime. For a number of reasons, these manifest functions have not been well achieved, but parole has acquired several latent functions which may be more responsible for its perpetuation than its official functions.

One latent or unofficial function of parole, of great impact in most correctional systems, is reduction of the disparity in punishments imposed by the courts. Sentencing practices of judges in different counties within a state, in different federal judicial districts, or even in different chambers of large multi-judge metropolitan courts, are highly diverse. Rural courts are usually severer than urban ones, but apart from this, each judge has a unique pattern in his use of the various sentencing alternatives available to him. Parole boards consist of a few people of diverse background (most frequently lawyers who have been active in politics), but they consider for parole virtually everyone sentenced in their state (or for the U.S. Board of Parole, those sentenced by all federal courts). Parole boards tend to be greatly preoccupied with "making the punishment fit the crime" and fit the criminal in a more consistent manner than do the original sentences of the many separate judges. A parole board's achievements in reduction of punishment disparity, however, are rarely proclaimed as the official objectives of their activity, for this function was never stressed in the ideology promoting establishment of parole.

A second highly important latent function of parole is the encouragement of inmate conformity to prison rules and to the authority of prison staff. Time is the most effective reward or punishment that the state has for regulating the behavior of its prisoners. In most prisons the wardens have authority to alter the duration of incarceration by approving or disapproving 5 to 25 percent off the sentence as a reward for good behavior, but a parole board usually has still greater power; the maximum duration of confinement it is permitted to impose is usually three to ten or more times the minimum to which it is constrained by statute. Research shows that conformity to prison discipline is not a highly accurate or consistent predictor of postrelease criminality; some avocational and crisis-vacillating offenders have a difficult time adjusting to institutional life, while some vocational predators are used to it and gain a reputation with wardens as "good prisoners." Nevertheless, if parole boards ignore variations of tractability during imprisonment the wardens lose one of their most effective arguments in persuading prisoners to conform, and they let parole boards know this. Indeed, any sudden tightening up of parole release policy has immediate repercussions in creating a tension among inmates that is highly conducive to riots, while any relaxation of release restrictions raises inmate morale and makes prison management easier.

A third important latent function of parole today is simply that of economy. Confinement costs about ten times as much per man-year as supervision on parole, so parole boards are quickly made aware of budgetary repercussions if they decrease the extent of parole, and they may be pressured to parole more liberally when institutions are crowded and correctional budgets are tight.

While the latent functions of parole persist, the manifest functions have never been very successfully achieved. Systematic research to determine the information most predictive of behavior on parole made it clear that observations of offenders in the unnatural conditions of prison life were not nearly as useful, when forecasting their adjustment in the free community, as information on their pre-prison lives (Glaser and O'Leary, 1966). Both assistance and surveillance of parolees have been relatively ineffective because of the large ratios of parolees to parole supervision staff, the priority which these staff give to paperwork rather than to field work, the social distance between staff and parolees, the limited resources for assistance, and some incompatibility between assistance and surveillance roles (Glaser, 1969). These conditions severely restrict the contribution of parole to reintegration of offenders. These limitations of traditional parole led to the growth, since the 1960s, of programs which involve less complete freedom and more extensive assistance in the community than occurs with parole or probation as they are usually administered.

Work release or *work furlough* consists of the daily release of prisoners to employment in the free community. It is usually permitted only near the end of a prison sentence, but often comprises all of a jail term.

Halfway houses were originally for homeless releasees from prisons and jails. They were usually operated by church-related private organizations rather than by the state. In their most effective form, pioneered by U.S. federal prisons in the 1960s, they are part of the government's correctional facilities for the last few months of imprisonment before parole. Called "community treatment centers," they often are in a wing of a metropolitan hotel or YMCA, and their residents arrive individually by public transportation from the prisons. After an initial day or two of visits by their families and orientation counseling, they go forth daily to seek work, or to employment when they have it, and are gradually given evening and weekend passes for recreation and visiting family. Often they move to their prospective homes before parole begins, but report to the center several times per week.

Counseling in work release or community correction has the advantage of dealing with immediate problems in employment or social relationships, rather than with abstractions perceived retrospectively or speculatively while still in prison. From the standpoint of surveillance to protect the public, close and frequent staff contact with the inmate while he is in the community daily permits more accurate diagnosis of his readiness for parole than is possible from observation in prison. Parole may be deferred or revoked, and the releasee returned to a regular prison, if he continually fails to pursue employment or persists in alcoholism or drug addiction that, in his career, are related to crime. If he reverts to crime it is usually known by authorities more quickly when he is on work release or at a community correctional residence than when he is released to live completely on his own as soon as he leaves the prison, under traditional parole conditions.

The differences between correctional staff and offenders are usually major impediments to effective counseling by staff. These differences of importance include social economic class, ethnicity and education, as well as experience in delinquency and crime. Such contrasts have been reduced by recruitment of ex-offenders as staff, especially those resident in the neighborhoods of the released offenders in community correctional programs. This staff change is perhaps most highly developed by the Los Angeles County Department of Probation. Their highest crime rate areas are staffed by numerous three-person teams, of which two members—called "Community Workers"—are from the neighborhood and usually ex-offenders, while the third member is a college-educated probation officer. The latter is often of middle class background, but is generally of the same ethnicity as most of his clientele. Each such team has a caseload of only thirty persons, with each member assigned ten but all available when needed for any of the thirty. Prior to this program, most of these probationers would have been institutionalized and not granted probation. The savings in institution expenses more than compensate for the cost of high staff to client ratios on probation. These teams operate from small centers scattered in the community and treat the entire family of each probationer as their concern. The community workers are available when needed at night and on weekends for every type of problem, from marital or parent-child conflict to overdoses of drugs, and from procuring employment to dealing with welfare or hospital authorities. By assisting in mundane matters—even housekeeping and babysitting in emergencies—bonds are developed between workers and clients which increase the influence of the workers. By exemplifying success at legitimate pursuits despite handicapped and stigmatized earlier lives, the workers—usually only slightly older than the probationers—are readily accepted as models of behavior by their clientele.

Community treatment centers may serve as "half-way in" residential centers in lieu of imprisonment, rather than as "half-way out" centers for release from prison. They provide temporary shelter for probationers, emergency housing and assistance centers for parolees experiencing crises, and also serve as centers for some offenders receiving intensive community correction services on a daily basis.

Guiding Correctional Policy

The primary deficiency of contemporary correction, from the standpoint of social policy, is the fact that it is not systematically and adequately guided by research. Failure to invest even 1 percent of correctional expenditures in research and failure to focus much research on measuring effectiveness means that correctional policy is determined more by expediency, custom, or unsystematic impressions of new procedures than by the demonstrated long-run effectiveness of correctional practices. In this respect correction is similar to much police and court operation.

One reason for the limited guidance of police, courts, and correction by the consequences of their actions for crime reduction is the fact that these three components of government are so autonomous. Intensifying traditional separation of judicial from executive branches of government is the fact that most police are organized in municipal units, courts are predominantly county, while prisons and parole are mainly state functions. Within adult correction the prison and parole administrations are often highly independent of each other.

As indicated earlier, assessment of police policy by arrests instead of by convictions fosters poor police work; similarly, assessment of correctional achievements by offender behavior during confinement instead of after release is a major cause of prison programs that pacify but do not rehabilitate.

The major thrust in correction as we enter the 1970s is in its community components, including probation, work release, and the community treatment centers of prison systems. The latter have provided a secondary benefit of informing prison administrators on the relevance of their vocational and other training programs to opportunities for ex-convicts in the free world. Optimum feedback in correction requires systematic and long-term statistical data-gathering on offender careers, with controled experimentation in correctional practice where possible (Glaser, 1971). This could provide all decision-makers—who must choose among sentence, correctional program, or parole date alternatives—with information on the probability of recidivism for every type of offender with each possible decision. Beginnings have been made in such research (Adams, 1967; Glaser, 1969), but they are only beginnings.

By projecting the trends described and analyzed in this book and by considering what support these trends receive from social science theory and research, one can anticipate three broad developments in reactions of the public and its governmental units to crime:

1. There will be continual redefinition of "crime" to limit offenses for which penalties are imposed to those which produce a definite victim. These offenses will be primarily what we have called predations, where the victimization is intentional, but they will also include a wide range of criminal negligence, such as recklessness in operating automobiles or other machines, and carelessness in manufacture or construction. Interest of the state in punishing people for what we have called performance, consumption, or selling offenses will diminish, and much of this activity that is now criminal will be legitimated. This trend is partly the result of growing tolerance for deviant behavior when it does not clearly victimize others (e.g., in sexual expression among consenting adults and in use of drugs). It is also because of increased recognition that agencies of the criminal justice system are relatively ineffective, create great inequities, and are readily corruptible when called upon to combat these types of deviance. Prominent evidence of such trends include use of medically oriented centers for voluntary detoxification instead of use of jails for drunkenness, defining homosexuality as an offense only if it involves an adult with a juvenile or use of force, the legalization of abortion, and more emphasis on regulation of drug distribution than on penal sanctions for drug possession. These trends will be accelerated by growing pressure to relieve congestion in the courts, overwork of the police, and crowded idleness in jails. All of these agencies are now heavily burdened by "victimless" offenses, especially drunkenness and marijuana cases.

2. There will be increased emphasis on certainty and speed, rather than on severity, whenever punishment is the primary government method of reaction to an offense. Punishment policies will be based increasingly upon controlled experiments to test effectiveness of penalties as general deterrents, rather than upon a passion for revenge. This emphasis on certainty of penalties will be restricted to offenses that are readily detected, and are committed very deliberately by persons without a great emotional stake in their criminal activity and with ample access to legitimate means for pursuing the economic or other objectives of their crimes. The offenses involved range from parking and drunken driving to fraudulent advertising and tax evasion. The "breathalyzer" aid to certainty of drunken driving

penalties, for example, appears clearly to promote caution in a drinker's choice of transportation, even though it probably has little effect on the prevalence of alcoholism.

3. Correctional measures for persistent offenders will become more diverse and flexible, varying according to the life history of the criminal much more than according to those particular offenses with which he is charged at any specific moment. The primary focus will be on facilitating success in legitimate alternatives to crime, and on making these alternatives more securely and profoundly gratifying than crime, rather than merely on restraining offenders for some duration of confinement. This means more concern with providing training and experience for legitimate employment, with monetary rewards to motivate initial self-help efforts. It also means more use of ex-offender staff, and locating correctional programs in the community rather than in confinement institutions, in order to give more social support to reformation and to cope with its problems where they must ultimately be solved, which is where the clientele of correction will live. This, however, may still involve use of traditional "firm, but fair" controls and appreciable periods of institutional confinement for the more professional criminals, for whom research shows counseling oriented and highly permissive programs at first have negative effects.

These three emerging trends represent the currently evolving stages of progress from revenge to rationality and sympathy in society's reaction to crime. This change is one of gradual evolution, with advances often offset by growth in conditions promoting crime, and by unanticipated deleterious consequences from what are presumed to be beneficial police, court, or correctional practices.

It is hoped that this book contributes to an awareness of the diversity of causal processes in crime, to a systematic view of criminal justice and correctional agencies, and to a continuing search for guidance through scientific methods of inquiry.

SELECTED REFERENCES

ABRAMS, ARNOLD, JOHN H. GAGNON, AND JOSEPH J. LEVIN
  1968 "Psychosocial aspects of addiction." *American Journal of Public Health* 58 (November): 2142–55.

ADAMS, STUART
  1967 "Some findings from correctional caseload research." *Federal Probation* 31 (December): 48–57.

———
  1970 "The PICO Project" in Norman Johnston, Leonard Savitz, and Marvin E. Wolfgang (eds.), *The Sociology of Punishment and Correction*, 2nd Ed., New York: John Wiley & Sons.

ALLEN, DAVID D.
  1952 *The Nature of Gambling.* New York: Coward-McCann, Inc.

ALLEN, HARRY E., LEWIS LINDNER, HAROLD GOLDMAN, AND SIMON DINITZ
  1969 "The social and bio-medical correlates of sociopathy." *Criminologica* 6 (February): 68–75.

AMERICAN PSYCHIATRIC ASSOCIATION, COMMITTEE ON NOMENCLATURE AND STATISTICS
  1963 *Diagnostic and Statistical Manual, Mental Disorders.* Washington: American Psychiatric Association.

ASCH, SOLOMON E.
    1952   "Effects of group pressures upon modification and distortion of judgments," in G. E. Swanson, T. M. Newcomb and E. L. Hartley, *Readings in Social Psychology*. New York: Holt, Rinehart & Winston, Inc.

BABST, DEAN V., JAMES A. INCIARDI, PHILIP K. RAEDER, JR., AND D. BARRI NEGRI
    1969   *Driving Records of Heroin Addicts*. Research Report No. 1969–11. Albany: New York State Department of Motor Vehicles.

BALL, JOHN C.
    1965   "Two patterns of narcotic addiction in the United States." *Journal of Criminal Law, Criminology and Police Science* 56 (June): 203–11.

BANFIELD, LAURA, AND C. DAVID ANDERSON
    1968   "Continuances in the Cook County Criminal Courts." *University of Chicago Law Review* 35 (Winter): 259–316.

BECKER, HOWARD S.
    1960   "Notes on the concept of commitment." *American Journal of Sociology* 66 (July): 32–40.

BITTNER, EGON
    1967   "The police on skid-row: A study of peace-keeping." *American Sociological Review* 32 (October): 699–715.

BLACK, DONALD J., AND ALBERT J. REISS, JR.
    1967   "Patterns of behavior in police and citizen transactions," Volume II, Section 1 of President's Commission on Law Enforcement and the Administration of Justice, Field Surveys III, *Studies in Law Enforcement in Major Metropolitan Areas*. Washington: U.S. Government Printing Office.

BLUM, RICHARD H., ASSISTED BY LAURAINE BRAUNSTEIN
    1967   "Mind-altering drugs and dangerous behavior: alcohol," Appendix B to President's Commission on Law Enforcement and Administration of Justice, *Task Force Report: Drunkenness*. Washington: U.S. Government Printing Office.

BLUMBERG, ABRAHAM S.
    1967   *Criminal Justice*. Chicago: Quadrangle Books, Inc.

BORDUA, DAVID J.
    1968   "Comments on police-community relations." *Connecticut Law Review* 1 (December): 306–31.

———, AND ALBERT J. REISS, JR.
    1967   "Law enforcement," in Paul Lazarsfeld, William H. Sewell and

Harold L. Wilensky (eds.), *The Uses of Sociology.* New York: Basic Books, Inc., Publishers.

BRIAR, SCOTT, AND IRVING PILIAVIN
1965 "Delinquency, situational inducements, and commitment to conformity." *Social Problems* 13 (Summer): 35–45.

BRYAN, JAMES H.
1965 "Apprenticeships in prostitution." *Social Problems* 12 (Winter): 287–97.

CAMERON, MARY OWENS
1964 *The Booster and the Snitch: Department Store Shoplifting.* New York: The Free Press.

CAPOTE, TRUMAN
1965 *In Cold Blood.* New York: Random House, Inc.

CARNEY, FRANCIS J.
1969 "Correctional research and correctional decision-making: Some problems and prospects." *Journal of Research on Crime and Delinquency* 6 (July): 110–22.

CATTELL, RAYMOND B.
1965 *The Scientific Analysis of Personality.* Baltimore, Md.: Penguin Books, Inc.

CHAMBLISS, WILLIAM J.
1967 "Types of deviance and the effectiveness of legal sanctions." *Wisconsin Law Review* 3 (Summer): 703–19.

CLARK, JOHN P.
1965 "Isolation of the police: A comparison of the British and American situations." *Journal of Criminal Law, Criminology, and Police Science* 56 (September): 307–19.

CLINARD, MARSHALL B., AND RICHARD QUINNEY
1967 *Criminal Behavior Systems: A Typology.* New York: Holt, Rinehart & Winston, Inc.

COHEN, HAROLD L., JAMES A. FILIPCZAK, JOHN S. BIS, AND JOAN E. COHEN
1966 *Contingencies Applicable to Special Education of Delinquents.* Silver Spring, Md.: Institute for Behavioral Research, Inc.

COLEMAN, JAMES S.
1961 *The Adolescent Society.* New York: The Free Press.

CRANCER, ALFRED, JAMES M. DILLE, JACK C. DELAY, JEAN E. WALLACE, AND MARTIN D. HOYKIN
1969 *The Effects of Marihuana and Alcohol on Simulated Driving Performances.* Olympia, Wash.: State Department of Motor Vehicles. (Also published in *Science,* May 16, 1969).

CRESSEY, DONALD R.
1953   *Other People's Money.* New York: The Free Press.

———
1969   *Theft of the Nation: The Structure and Operations of Organized Crime in America.* New York: Harper & Row, Publishers.

CUMMING, ELAINE, IAN CUMMING, AND LAURA EDELL
1965   "Policeman as philosopher, guide and friend." *Social Problems* 12 (Winter) : 276–86.

DOLE, VINCENT P., MARIE E. NYSWANDER, AND ALAN WARNER
1968   "Successful treatment of 750 criminal addicts." *Journal of the American Medical Association* 206 (December 16) : 2709–711.

DRIVER, EDWIN D.
1968   "A critique of typologies in criminology." *Sociological Quarterly* 9 (Summer) : 356–73.

ELLIOTT, DELBERT S.
1966   "Delinquency, school attendance and dropout." *Social Problems* 13 (Winter) : 307–14.

EYSENCK, H. J.
1964   *Crime and Personality.* Boston: Houghton Mifflin Company.

FERDINAND, THEODORE N.
1967   "The criminal patterns of Boston since 1849." *American Journal of Sociology* 73 (July) : 84–99.

FINESTONE, HAROLD
1957   "Cats, kicks and color." *Social Problems* 5 (July) : 3–13.

———
1967   "Reformation and recidivism among Italian and Polish criminals." *American Journal of Sociology* 72 (May) : 575–88.

FREEMAN, LINTON C., AND ROBERT F. WINCH
1957   "Societal complexity: An empirical test of a typology of societies." *American Journal of Sociology* 62 (March) : 461–66.

GARDNER, JOHN A., WITH THE ASSISTANCE OF DAVID J. OLSON
1967   "Wincanton: The Politics of Corruption," Appendix B of President's Commission for Law Enforcement and the Administration of Justice. *Task Force Report: Organized Crime.* Washington: U.S. Government Printing Office, 61–79.

GEBHARD, PAUL H., JOHN H. GAGNON, WARDELL B. POMEROY, AND CORNELIA V. CHRISTENSON
1965   *Sex Offenders.* New York: Harper & Row, Publishers.

GIBBONS, DON C.
1968   *Society, Crime and Criminal Careers.* Englewood Cliffs, N.J.: Prentice-Hall, Inc.

GLASER, DANIEL

1962   "The differential-association theory of crime" in Arnold M.
        Rose (ed.), *Human Behavior and Social Processes.* Boston,
        Mass.: Houghton Mifflin Company.

1967   "National Goals and Indicators for the Reduction of Crime and
        Delinquency." *Annals of the American Academy of Political
        and Social Science* 371 (May): 104–26.

1968   "Penology," in *International Encyclopedia of the Social Sci-
        ences.* New York: The Macmillan Company.

1969   *The Effectiveness of a Prison and Parole System* (abridged
        edition). Indianapolis, Ind.: The Bobbs-Merrill Company, Inc.

1970   "Some notes on urban jails," in Daniel Glaser (ed.), *Crime in
        the City.* New York: Harper & Row, Publishers.

1971   "Five practical research suggestions for correctional administra-
        tors." *Crime and Delinquency* 17 (January): 32–40.

———, AND JOHN R. STRATTON

1961   "Measuring inmate change in prison," in Donald R. Cressey
        (ed.), *The Prison: Studies in Institutional Organization and
        Change.* New York: Holt, Rinehart & Winston, Inc.

———, FRED COHEN, AND VINCENT O'LEARY

1966   *The Sentencing and Parole Process.* Washington, D.C.: U.S.
        Government Printing Office.

———, DONALD KENEFICK, AND VINCENT O'LEARY

1966   *The Violent Offender. Washington,* D.C.: U.S. Government
        Printing Office.

———, AND VINCENT O'LEARY

1966   *Personal Characteristics and Parole Outcome.* Washington,
        D.C.: U.S. Government Printing Office.

———, AND MARY SNOW

1969   *Public Knowledge and Attitudes on Drug Abuse in New York
        State.* Albany, N.Y.: New York State Narcotic Addiction Con-
        trol Commission.

———, BERNARD LANDER, AND WILLIAM ABBOTT

1971   "Opiate addicted and non-addicted siblings in a slum area."
        Social Problems (in press).

GOLDSTEIN, HERMAN
  1963   "Police discretion: The ideal vs. the real." *Public Administration Review* 23 (September) : 140–48.

_____
  1967   "Administrative problems in controlling the exercise of police authority." *Journal of Criminal Law, Criminology and Police Science* 58 (June) : 160–72.

_____
  1968   "Trial judges and the police: Their relationship in the administration of criminal justice." *Crime and Delinquency* 14 (January) : 14–25.

GOLDSTEIN, JOSEPH
  1960   "Police discretion not to invoke the criminal process: Low visibility decisions in the administration of justice." *Yale Law Journal* 69 (March) : 543–88.

GRANT, J. DOUGLAS, AND MARGUERITE Q. GRANT
  1959   "A group dynamics approach to the treatment of nonconformists in the Navy." *Annals of the American Academy of Political and Social Science,* 322 (March) : 126–35.

HALL, JEROME
  1952   *Theft, Law and Society* (2nd ed.). Indianapolis, Ind.: The Bobbs-Merrill Company, Inc.

HALL, REIS H., MILDRED MILAZZO, AND JUDY POSNER
  1966   *A Descriptive and Comparative Study of Recidivism in Pre-Release Guidance Center Releasees.* Washington, D.C.: U.S. Department of Justice, Bureau of Prisons.

HUTT, PETER BARTON
  1967   "The recent court decisions on alcoholism: A challenge to the North American Judges Association and its members." Appendix H to President's Commission on Law Enforcement and the Administration of Justice, *Task Force Report: Drunkenness.* Washington, D.C.: U.S. Government Printing Office.

IRWIN, JOHN
  1970   *The Felon.* Englewood Cliffs, N.J.: Prentice-Hall, Inc.

JAFFE, JEROME H., MISHA S. ZAKS, AND EDWARD N. WASHINGTON
  1969   "Experience with the use of methadone in a multi-modality program for the treatment of narcotics users." *International Journal of the Addictions* 4 (September) : 481–90.

JAMES, RITA M.
  1959   "Status and competence of jurors." *American Journal of Sociology* 64 (May) : 563–70.

KOVAL, MARY
   1969   *Opiate Use in New York City.* New York: New York State
          Narcotic Addiction Control Commission, Research Division.

KRAMER, JOHN C., AND RICHARD A. BASS
   1969   "Institutionalization patterns among civilly committed addicts."
          Journal of the American Medical Association 208 (June 23):
          2297–301.

LAFAVE, WAYNE R.
   1965   *Arrest: The Decision to Take a Suspect Into Custody.* Boston,
          Mass.: Little, Brown and Company.

LAW ENFORCEMENT ASSISTANCE ADMINISTRATION
   1970   *The St. Louis Detoxification and Diagnostic Evaluation Center.*
          Washington, D.C.: U.S. Government Printing Office.

LEMERT, EDWIN M.
   1967   *Human Deviance, Social Problems and Social Control.* Engle-
          wood Cliffs, N.J.: Prentice-Hall, Inc.

LEWIS, MICHAEL
   1970   "Structural deviance and normative conformity: The 'hustle'
          and the gang," in Daniel Glaser (ed.), *Crime in the City.* New
          York: Harper & Row, Publishers.

LINDESMITH, ALFRED R.
   1965   *The Addict and the Law.* Bloomington, Ind.: Indiana Univer-
          sity Press.

LOPREATO, JOSEPH, AND LETITIA ALSTON
   1970   "Ideal types and idealization strategy." *American Sociological
          Review* 35 (February): 88–96.

MARSHALL, JAMES
   1966   *Law and Psychology in Conflict.* Indianapolis, Ind.: The Bobbs-
          Merrill Company, Inc.

MATZA, DAVID
   1964   *Delinquency and Drift.* New York: John Wiley & Sons, Inc.

MAURER, DAVID W.
   1940   *The Big Con.* New York: Signet Books.

————
   1964   *Whiz Mob.* New Haven, Conn.: College and University Press.

MAXWELL, MILTON A.
   1962   "Alcoholics Anonymous: An interpretation," in David J. Pitt-
          man and Charles R. Snyder (eds.), *Society, Culture and Drink-
          ing Patterns.* New York: John Wiley & Sons, Inc.

McKEE, JOHN M.
   1968   "Methods of motivating offenders," in *Proceedings of the 97th*

Annual Congress of Correction, 1967. Washington, D.C.: American Correctional Association.

MECHANIC, DAVID
1970 *Mental Health and Social Policy.* Englewood Cliffs, N.J.: Prentice-Hall, Inc.

MISNER, GORDON E.
1960 "Recent developments in the metropolitan law enforcement." *Journal of Criminal Law, Criminology and Police Science* 50 (February), 497–508.

MORRIS, ALBERT
1965 "The comprehensive classification of adult offenders." *Journal of Criminal Law, Criminology and Police Science* 56 (June): 197–202.

MORRIS, NORVAL, AND GORDON HAWKINS
1970 *The Honest Politician's Guide to Crime Control.* Chicago, Ill.: University of Chicago Press.

MORTON-WILLIAMS, R.
1962 "The relations between the police and the public," Appendix IV to Royal Commission on the Police, *Minutes of Evidence.* London: Her Majesty's Stationary Office.

NEWMAN, DONALD J.
1966 *Conviction: The Determination of Guilt or Innocence Without Trial.* Boston, Mass.: Little, Brown and Company.

NEWTON, GEORGE D., AND FRANKLIN E. ZIMRING
1969 *Firearms and Violence in American Life.* Report No. 7 to the National Commission on the Causes and Prevention of Violence. Washington, D.C.: U.S. Government Printing Office.

O'DONNELL, JOHN A.
1965 "The relapse rate in narcotic addiction: A critique of follow-up studies," in Daniel M. Wilner and Gene G. Kassebaum (eds.), *Narcotics.* New York: McGraw-Hill Book Company.

——— 1966 "Narcotic addition and crime." *Social Problems* 13 (Spring): 374–85.

OHLIN, LLOYD E., AND FRANK J. REMINGTON
1958 "Sentencing structure: Its effect upon systems for the administration of criminal justice." *Law and Contemporary Problems* 23 (Summer): 495–507.

PARSONS, TALCOTT
1951 *The Social System.* New York: The Free Press.

PETTIGREW, THOMAS F., AND ROSALIND B. SPIER
  1962   "The ecological structure of Negro homicide." *American Journal of Sociology* 67 (May): 621–29.

PITTMAN, DAVID J., AND WILLIAM HANDY
  1964   "Patterns in criminal aggravated assault." *Journal of Criminal Law, Criminology and Police Science* 55 (December): 462–70.

PLATT, ANTHONY
  1969   *The Child Savers: The Invention of Delinquency.* Chicago, Ill.: University of Chicago Press.

POWNALL, GEORGE A.
  1969   *Employment Problems of Released Prisoners.* Washington, D.C.: Manpower Administration, U.S. Department of Labor.

PRESIDENT'S COMMISSION ON LAW ENFORCEMENT AND THE ADMINISTRATION OF JUSTICE
  1967   *The Challenge of Crime in a Free Society.* Washington, D.C.: U.S. Government Printing Office.

PRICE, HUGH B.
  1968   "A proposal for handling of petty misdemeanor offenses." *Connecticut Bar Journal* 42 (March): 55–74.

REISS, ALBERT J., JR.
  1968   "Police brutality—answers to key questions." *Trans-action* 5 (August): 10–19.

ROSS, H. LAURENCE, DONALD T. CAMPBELL, AND GENE V. GLASS
  1970   "Determining the social effects of a legal reform: the British 'Breathalyzer' Crackdown of 1967." *American Behavioral Scientist* 13 (March/April): 493–509.

SCHUR, EDWIN M.
  1969   *Our Criminal Society: The Social and Legal Sources of Crime in America.* Englewood Cliffs, N.J.: Prentice-Hall, Inc.

SELLIN, THORSTEN, ED.
  1967   *Capital Punishment.* New York: Harper & Row, Publishers.

————, AND MARVIN E. WOLFGANG
  1964   *The Measurement of Delinquency.* New York: John Wiley & Sons, Inc.

SHORT, JAMES F., JR., AND FRED L. STRODTBECK
  1965   *Group Process and Gang Delinquency.* Chicago, Ill.: University of Chicago Press.

SKOLNICK, JEROME H.
  1966   *Justice Without Trial: Law Enforcement in Democratic Society.* New York: John Wiley & Sons, Inc.

SMIGEL, ERWIN O.
   1956   "Public attitudes toward stealing as related to the size of the victim organization." *American Sociological Review* 21 (June): 320–27.
——, AND H. LAURENCE ROSS
   1970   *Crimes Against Bureaucracy.* New York: Van Nostrand Reinhold Company.
STODDARD, ELWYN R.
   1968   "The informal 'code' of police deviance: A group approach to 'Blue Coat Crime.'" *Journal of Criminal Law, Criminology and Political Science* 59 (June): 201–13.
STRODBECK, FRED L., RITA M. JAMES, AND CHARLES HAWKINS
   1957   "Social status in jury deliberations." *American Sociological Review* 22 (December): 713–19.
SUDNOW, DAVID
   1965   "Normal crimes: Sociological features of the penal code in a public defender office." *Social Problems* 12 (Winter): 255–76.
SUTHERLAND, EDWIN H.
   1949   *White Collar Crime.* New York: The Dryden Press, Inc.
SUTTER, ALAN G.
   1969   "Worlds of drug use on the street scene," in Donald R. Cressey and David A. Ward (eds.), *Delinquency, Crime and Social Process.* New York: Harper & Row, Publishers.
SYKES, GRESHAM M.
   1958   *The Society of Captives: A Study of a Maximum Security Prison.* Princeton, N.J.: Princeton University Press.
TOCH, HANS H.
   1969   *Violent Men.* Chicago, Ill.: Aldine Publishing Company.
VOSS, HARWIN L., AND JOHN R. HEPBURN
   1968   "Patterns in criminal homicide in Chicago." *Journal of Criminal Law, Criminology and Police Science* 59 (December): 499–508.
WALDO, GORDON P., AND SIMON DINITZ
   1967   "Personality attributes of the criminal." *Journal of Research in Crime and Delinquency* 4 (July): 185–202.
WALKER, NIGEL
   1965   *Crime and Punishment in Britain.* Edinburgh, Scotland: The University Press.
WEIL, ANDREW T., NORMAN E. ZINBERG, AND JUDITH M. NELSEN
   1968   "Clinical and psychological effects of marihuana in man." *Science* 162 (December 13): 1234–242.

WERTHMAN, CARL

    1967   "The function of social definitions in the development of criminal careers," Appendix J of President's Commission on Law Enforcement and the Administration of Justice, *Task Force Report: Juvenile Delinquency*. Washington, D.C.: U.S. Government Printing Office.

WESTLEY, WILLIAM A.

    1953   "Violence and the police." *American Journal of Sociology* 49 (August): 34–41.

———

    1956   "Secrecy and the police." *Social Forces* 31 (March): 254–55.

WILEY, NORBERT

    1967   "The ethnic mobility trap and stratification theory." *Social Problems* 15 (Fall): 147–59.

WILSON, JAMES Q.

    1968   *Varieties of Police Behavior*. Cambridge, Mass.: Harvard University Press.

WINCH, ROBERT F.

    1947   "Heuristic and empirical typologies: A job for factor analysis." *American Sociological Review* 12 (February): 68–75.

WINICK, CHARLES

    1961   "Physician narcotic addicts." *Social Problems* 9 (Fall): 174–86.

WOLFGANG, MARVIN E.

    1958   *Patterns in Criminal Homicide*. Philadelphia, Pa.: University of Pennsylvania Press.

———, AND FRANCO FERRACUTI

    1967   *The Subculture of Violence*. London, England: Tavistock Publications.

YABLONSKY, LEWIS

    1964   *Synanon: The Tunnel Back*. New York: The Macmillan Company.

ZEIZEL, HANS

    1969   "Methodological problems in studies of sentencing." *Law and Society Review* 3 (May): 621–31.

INDEX

INDEX

Accusatorial procedure, 81
Addiction-supporting predators, 37–43, 103
Adolescence, 8–12, 28–31
Adolescence recapitulators, 28–31, 105
Adulthood, 1–2, 10–12
Adversary system, 81
Age, and crime or delinquency, 1–2, 4–6, 8–12, 41
Alcoholics Anonymous, 41–42
Alcoholism, and crime, 25, 37–38, 40, 63–64, 66, 110–11
Amphetamines, 37, 64–65
Arraignment, 95
Arrest, 6, 71–74, 82, 84–85, 89–90
Arson, 16
Assault, 3, 6–7, 21, 32–36
Auburn System, 103
Auto theft, 6, 29, 31
Avocational predators, 56–58, 105

Bail, 87–91
Barbiturates, 37, 64–65

Bill of Rights, 71–72, 85–86. *See also* Constitution of the United States, first ten amendments
Bondsmen, 89–90
Bowery Project, 64
Bunco. *See* Confidence game
Burglary, 3, 5–7, 46

Capital Punishment, 35–36
Commitment, 11, 19–26, 29
Community correction, 31, 107–9, 111
Confidence game, 3, 21, 44–46
Constitution of the United States
    Second Amendment, 36
    Fourth Amendment, 71, 72
    Fifth Amendment, 71
    Sixth Amendment, 71
    Fourteenth Amendment, 72
    Eighteenth Amendment, 4
    Twenty-first Amendment, 4
Continuances, 91–94, 97–98
Correction, 100–111

Cosa Nostra, 50–51
Counsel, right to, 72, 82–83
Counseling, 105, 108–9
Courts, 80–99
  history, 80–81
  procedure, 81–98
  reform, 98–99
  types, 81
Crime
  against persons, 3, 5, 15
  against property, 3, 5, 15
  age and, 1, 2, 4–6, 8–12
  causation, 8–65
  conflict and, 21
  definition, 1, 2–4
  distribution, 5–6
  politics and, 49–50
  prevention, 28, 30–31, 36, 43, 47
  statistics, 5–7
Criminal negligence, 4, 6, 17
Crisis-vacillation predators, 58–59, 105
Culture. *See* Subcultures

Defense counsel, 82–84, 92–93
Delay in court, 91–94, 97–98
Delinquency. *See* Juvenile delinquency
Deterrence, 57, 102–3, 111
Disorderly conduct, 4, 6
Drugs. *See* Narcotics
Drunkenness, 5–6, 62–64, 110–11. *See*
  Alcoholism

Education
  and crime, 28–29, 30–31, 34, 36
  in prison, 104
Embezzlement, 3, 6, 21, 58–59
Employment, and crime, 20, 30–31, 36,
  104
Escobedo v. *Illinois,* 72
Exclusionary rule, 72

Federal Bureau of Investigation, 6, 68
Felony, 94, 95
Fines, 35, 102
Firearms, and crime rates, 35–36
Forgery, 3, 6, 18, 21, 38
Fraud, 3, 5, 6. *See also* Confidence game,
  Embezzlement, Forgery

Gambling, 4, 6, 48, 52–54
Gideon v. *Wainwright,* 72
Goring, Charles, 24
Grand Jury, 94–95

Habeas corpus, 82
Heroin, 39–43
Homicide, 4, 6, 32–34. *See also* Man-
  slaughter, Murder
Homosexuality, 65–66

Illegal consumption, 3–4, 5, 16–17
Illegal performance, 4, 5, 17
Illegal selling, 3–4, 5, 16–17, 47–56
Indecent liberties. *See* Sexual molestation
Index offenses, 6
Initial appearance, 81–91
Inquisitorial procedure, 81
Italians, and organized crime, 50–51

Jails, 94, 104–5
Juvenile court, 2
Juvenile delinquency
  definition, 2
  relation to adult crime, 4–5, 10–12, 28–31
Juvenile status offenses, 2
Jury. *See* Trial Jury, Grand Jury

Kidnapping, 3

Labelling, 10
Larceny. *See* Theft
Loan-sharking, 48, 54–55
Lombroso, Cesare, 24
LSD, 37, 64

Mafia, 50
Manslaughter, 4, 6
Mapp v. *Ohio,* 72
Marijuana, 10, 37, 40–41, 64–65

Methadone, 42–43, 55
Miranda v. *Arizona,* 72
Misdemeanor, 94, 95
Mobility trap, 29
Morphine, 38
Murder
  causation, 21, 32–36, 47
  definition, 3, 4
  professional, 47, 49, 51
  quasi-insane, 60–61
  statistics, 6, 32–36

Narcotics, 6, 18, 21, 38–43, 48, 64–66, 110.
  See also Addiction-supporting pred-
  ators, Amphetamines, Barbiturates,
  Heroin, Marijuana, Methadone,
  Opiates, Private illegal consumers
Negotiated justice, 81–82, 83–84, 89, 95
Nonage, 1–2

Opiates, 38–43, 55
Order Maintenance, 70–71
Organized illegal sellers, 47–56

Paranoia, 25–26, 103
Parens patriae, 2
Parental relationships, and crime, 30
Parole, 101, 106–7
Peacekeeping, 70–71
Peel, Sir Robert, 68
Pennsylvania System, 103
Personality, and crime, 23–26
Petit Jury, 95–97
Pickpocketing, 44, 46
Pilfering, 57
Police, 67–79, 84–87
  clearance rate, 73, 87
  concerns, 69
  court regulation, 84–87, 99
  discretion, 69–71, 73–74, 77–78
  history, 67–68
  public relations, 75–79
  styles, 74–75
Posse comitatus, 68
Powell v. *Texas,* 63
Predation, 2–3, 5, 15, 17–18, 29, 80, 110.
  See also, Addiction-supporting pred-

Predation (*continued*)
  ators, Avocational predators, Crisis-
  vacillation predators, Quasi-insane
  assaulters, Sub-cultural assaulters,
  Vocational predators
Preliminary hearing, 94, 95
Pretrial employment, 90–91
Prior criminal record, 19–20
Private illegal consumers, 64–66
Probation, 102, 108–9
Professional criminals, 44–47
Prohibition, 4, 43, 48, 51, 52, 55–56
Prostitution, 4, 5–6, 18, 55–56
Psychopathy, 24–25
Public defender, 83
Punishment, 1, 35–36, 102–3, 110

Quasi-insane assaulters, 59–62

Racketeering, 49
Rape, 3, 6–7, 61
Recidivism, 11, 19–20, 104
Reckless driving. *See* Criminal negligence
Recognizance, 88, 90
Reformatories, 103
Relative deprivation-differential
  anticipation theory, 40, 43
Restitution, 102
Robbery, 3, 6–7, 15–16, 46
Robinson v. *California,* 41

Sanity and crime, 60
Sentencing, 100–102
Sexual molestation, 3, 61–62
Shoplifting, 18, 21, 46–47, 56–57
Social relationships, and crime, 20–22,
  29–30, 104–5
Social types, 13–14
Subcultural assaulters, 32–36
Subcultures, 9–10, 22, 44
St. Louis Detoxification and Diagnostic
  Evaluation Center, 64
Summons, 90
Symbiosis, and crime, 21–22, 46

Theft, 3, 5–7, 18. *See also,* Auto theft,
  Pickpocketing, Pilfering, Shoplifting

Trial Jury, 95–97
Typification, 12–14, 27–66

Usury, 48, 54, 55

Vagrancy, 4, 6
Veniremen, 95–96
Vera Foundation, 64, 90

Victims, 5–7, 32–34, 57, 78–79, 102
Victim survey research, 5–6, 78–79
Violence, 32–36. *See also,* Assault, Murder,
      Rape
Vocational predators, 44–47, 103, 105

Warrants, 72, 82
White collar crime, 57–58
Workhouses, 103
Work release, 107–8